I'm Mostly
Here to
Enjoy Myself

life

ALSO BY GLYNNIS MACNICOL

No One Tells You This

I'm Mostly Here to Enjoy Myself

ONE WOMAN'S PURSUIT
OF PLEASURE IN PARIS

GLYNNIS MacNICOL

PENGUIN LIFE

VIKING
An imprint of Penguin Random House LLC
penguinrandomhouse.com

A Penguin Life Book

LIBRARY OF CONGRESS CATALOGING-IN-PUBLICATION

Names: MacNicol, Glynnis, 1974– author.
Title: I'm mostly here to enjoy myself : one woman's pursuit of
pleasure in Paris / Glynnis MacNicol.
Other titles: One woman's pursuit of pleasure in Paris
Description: [New York] : Penguin Life, [2024] |
Identifiers: LCCN 2023054131 | ISBN 9780593655757 (hardcover) |
ISBN 9780593655764 (ebook)
Subjects: LCSH: MacNicol, Glynnis, 1974– —Travel—France—Paris. |
Americans—France—Paris. | Women authors, American—Biography. |
Pleasure. | Paris (France)—Description and travel.
Classification: LCC DC705.M33 A3 2024 | DDC 944/.004130092
[B]—dc23/eng/20240212
LC record available at https://lccn.loc.gov/2023054131

Printed in the United States of America
1st Printing

Set in Bell MT Pro
Designed by Cassandra Garruzzo Mueller

Some names and identifying characteristics have been changed to protect the privacy of the individuals involved.

For C.A.R. & E., my favorite fruitz

ces soirées là

Contents

I couldn't get what I wanted any other way so I've been painting myself—no clothes—It was lots of fun.

GEORGIA O'KEEFFE TO ALFRED STIEGLITZ, 1917

Our author, then, was one of many, and must be seen within the broad outlines of the moment in history of which she was a part.

MARGARET ATWOOD, THE HANDMAID'S TALE

Tomorrow I will take a long siesta.

ROMY SCHNEIDER, LA PISCINE

À Paris

On Sunday I spend a sunny hour in the Jardin des Plantes, sitting on one of the benches that line the long promenade, under trees that stand like sentinels. It's the fifteenth day of August 2021. I have been in Paris for just over two weeks. Overhead the sky is blue, the light filtering through the trees is golden and gentle. On my phone are messages I have exchanged with a man whose name and face I do not know. We matched on a French dating app shortly after I arrived. His profile has no photo, just a silhouette, and his age, forty-nine.

After we match, he immediately messages to tell me he is open-minded, six foot one, and fit. He tells me about the hourly hotels in Paris, ones accessible via an app I've never heard of, which make their rooms available during the afternoon between checkout and check-in. They all seem to be located near the Châtelet Métro station, in the center of the city. After two weeks of silence—he's been away on holiday—he's reappeared in my messages and asked if I would meet him over in the 6th for a drink. A let's see if we want to take our clothes off and be open-minded together assessment. This is at odds with many of the other proposals I've been receiving in the weeks since Silhouette and I first connected. The ones who simply want me to come over. To arrive without any underclothes on. To be waiting naked on my bed, the front door left unlocked. To be blindfolded. Tied up. Spanked. "What if we aren't attracted to one another," I say to these bolder requests. "There's always that chance," they tell me. Even through the broken English, I can feel the implied shrug. The very French absence of humor. Their lack of concern emanates through the screen. I don't need a translation: It's been a long year of little touch, it says. Physical attraction right now seems less a gamble than a given. Everyone is feral for connection.

When I first encountered Silhouette's profile, I had only just landed in Paris, and the lack of information struck me as refreshingly mysterious. It allowed me to sketch the details in myself. Exert more control, and anticipation, over who might be on the other end. But over the following weeks I realize, this silhouette business is not an uncommon practice: the French are notoriously obsessed with privacy. If I want actual photos, numbers need to be exchanged and the conversation moved to a presumably better-guarded WhatsApp. If it had been a week or two later, I wouldn't have bothered swiping, but I was still figuring it all out when I came across him.

I haven't responded to his request yet. Instead, I open my camera and look at myself. The light on my face reflects the way I feel—vibrant and compelling. Alive. My dating app bio says, "New Yorker, 46, à Paris pour un mois." It does not say, "I have been alone, untouched, in a very small apartment for fourteen months. Have hurled myself across the ocean amidst an increasingly uncertain summer to Paris, simply because I could." What's become apparent is that one result of suffering on a global scale is no one wants to talk about it. In the first weeks of March 2020 there was much puzzling over why we didn't have more stories about the 1918 flu pandemic. But now it seems clear: people want to move on as quickly as possible.

I read Silhouette's message again, contemplating whether I want to leave here and make my way over to the 6th, a full *arrondissement* away, to meet with a literal mystery man. I look around at the people walking the gravel paths. The parks in Paris each have a different personality. Monceau is full of joggers but rarely tourists. Luxembourg is like Central Park, too beautiful and central to be avoided by Parisians but overwhelmed by visitors. Buttes-Chaumont is for the youth. Here in Jardin des Plantes are the forty-something, well-dressed Parisians, secure in their lives and their attractiveness. They are established. They have dinner parties. They stroll. They have frolicking children. Normally you'd have to look for them through the tourists. But there are no tourists this year. There are only the French. And now there is me.

The truth is, I'm not especially curious what Silhouette looks like; either there will be attraction or there won't. I'm more excited to be seen. The long months of not being regarded. Not having my physical presence responded to even in the smallest ways—no one has touched me or even *smelled* me for over a year—has inadvertently stripped away the lifelong habit of itemizing all the things that are wrong with me before I present myself to the world. I don't care what might be wrong with me. Or rather, I can't seem to make myself care even when I try. I'm reminded of a time when I had a chest infection that resulted in such a deep, persistent cough the doctor prescribed me syrup that contained some type of morphine. When the urge to cough arrived, I found I simply couldn't. The body and the brain had been disconnected.

My body and brain are still very much tied together, but the former is currently running the show. And my body is not here for validation. My body is here for pleasure.

I decide to go. It's a beautiful day and I have nothing to lose.

I type back that I'm on my way.

I don't type *"en route,"* as I might have in any other circumstance or place because Ellie, a new friend in Paris and ten years my junior, has told me to never speak French to French men on dating apps. She tells me French men think less of you when you attempt their language, and the power dynamic shifts. I wonder if it's simply a matter of wanting what we don't normally have and, if this *is* the case, what is the experience like for non-English-speaking visitors in Paris? Who is rewarded for a language and who is punished and in what circumstances? Avoiding French is not exactly a huge challenge for me; at the best of times, my French is broken and my comprehension hit-and-miss. Even so, from time to time I slip in the odd *oui* or *avec plaisir.* It is sometimes easier to say what I mean in a language I don't really speak.

Paris is its own silhouette. If people hang their vague aspirations of ambition on New York, hoping the city will fuel their rise, or at least transform them into a person capable of rising, they do the same with their dreams of romance in Paris. The city is the masked figure everyone is swiping right on. There is apparently a condition called

Paris syndrome, coined by a Japanese psychiatrist named Hiroaki Ota in the eighties. It's supposedly primarily experienced by visitors from the eastern parts of Asia, particularly women in their thirties, who arrive in Paris and are deeply disappointed to discover the city does not live up in any way to its reputation. The symptoms of Paris syndrome, possibly apocryphal, are apparently so severe the Japanese embassy at one point set up a hotline for tourists to call so they could be immediately shipped home.

Certainly, one of the benefits of being in your forties must be the knowledge that depending on anything external to fundamentally transform you is a fool's errand. As my friend Nina likes to say, wherever you go, that's where you are. But looking to a city, or a dress, or a meal, or a person to throw a different light on things? To raise you up slightly from where you are and place you gently down a little way away so that everything looks familiar but perhaps a little taller? A little softer? A little stronger? More enjoyable? That's just good decision-making.

That's what I'm here for. I've had the same view of things for more than a year. Myself included. I want to see things differently. Myself most of all.

I close my messages with Silhouette; I'll know soon enough what's behind the blank outline. I get off the bench, stretch, snap one last glowing selfie in the dappled golden light, and begin my slow Sunday afternoon walk across empty Paris.

ONE

The Only Thing to Do Is Go

purchase my plane ticket to Paris in May of 2021, when everything in New York begins to feel possible again. The cold pandemic winter, the second one, is dissolving into a promising spring. Vaccines have staggered onto the scene. The new roaring twenties are soon to be upon us, goes the refrain. There is almost no evidence of this . . . yet. But it all *sounds* wonderful.

I have been alone for more than a year. Home Alone in New York. I see people, of course, but from a distance. My apartment building, all seventeen floors and three hundred plus apartments, emptied out so quickly during that single week in March of 2020, that I sometimes open my door and see mice scurrying across the hallways. "People took their cats with them," Cedric the exterminator tells me, by way of explanation. He is still doing his rounds around the city, running faucets in the spectacular, now dark, pre-wars that line Fifth Avenue so that the water bugs don't take over. In New York, water bugs are what we call enormous, three-inch-long cockroaches, thus named because they are drawn to water. They sometimes scurry up the radiator pipes in the winter, lured by the drops of condensation.

These are some of the many things I learn from Cedric, who also advises me to keep my toilet lid shut so that rats don't come up through the pipes. He says they are extra hungry now that there's no restaurant garbage. "But I'm on the seventeenth floor!" I protest. He shrugs. "They come up one floor, they take a rest. They go up the next floor." He hunches his shoulders and hooks his hands in front of him, imitating a rat tunneling up the ancient pipes of the building and presumably into my 450-square-foot studio, where it will no doubt eat my face while I sleep. A week or so later I look out my window and see a red-tailed hawk soaring by, a rat gripped tightly in its talons, its long, scaly rat tail swaying behind in the wind. I say a brief, silent prayer on the hawk's behalf that he or she is not about to have a meal laced with rat poison. For a number of months in 2020, Cedric is the only person I speak to regularly in real life.

I'm not the only person in the building. My next-door neighbor, who bought her similarly sized studio in the midnineties for $140,000 (a fifth of what it would sell for now), has remained and sometimes I hear her yell at her cat to get off the kitchen counter. The hoarder down the hall has also stayed; her TV blares *Law & Order: SVU* episodes day and night. Ray, the doorman, tells me that they think there's still an elderly woman on the thirteenth floor. Someone is up there ordering delivery. Ray's wife is a nurse at a hospital in Long Island, and for about six months last year she worked without a single day off.

But now it's spring. Our second pandemic spring. The tree in the dip beyond the 79th Street entrance to Riverside Park, where the path forks, has become my clock. In the fall, I watched it flame out in a blaze of gold glory, burst back in an explosion of pink six months later, and flame out once more. Now it is rosying up again. Over in Central Park, there are rumors that the chipmunks have been pushed back to the northern half of the park by all the rats—I'm told this when I do my park volunteer shift, spending hours a week silently raking up leaves, masked and gloved. But the city is slowly returning; I begin to notice there are more lights on in the buildings at night when I go for my walk along Central Park West up to 90th Street and back. There is once again a sprinkling of diners at outside tables. SoHo during the day no longer feels like a potential murder scene. There is the distinct sense people are reemerging, like the rows of tulip bulbs pushing up at the corners of the park. Life is returning.

Running with this energy, I dash off a quick email to the man who owns the apartment in Paris that I've rented in summers past—a past that belongs to another lifetime it seems now—asking if by chance the apartment is available. I expect nothing to come of it—they have only just announced the EU is thinking of opening its borders to vaccinated tourists this summer, but nothing is yet official—but just the act of writing it gives me a renewed sense of life. To my surprise he responds almost immediately: "It's so crazy, it just might work!" Five days later, he follows up with dates. August 1 to September 8. "Would that work?"

"Absolument," I reply just as quickly.

Anything works, really. Plans seem to belong not just to another lifetime, but to another timeline. Years of bumper stickers and Instagram accounts encouraging us to live in the now have not, it seems, prepared anyone to actually exist in a present where the future is so glaringly shifting like cursed quicksand in a fairy tale.

Possibly because of this uncertainty, I promptly send half the €1,100 it will cost to take the place for just over five weeks. A deposit to demonstrate I'm serious. But also to provide some sort of concrete connection to the future. Tie myself in recognizable ways to potential instead of being pinned down the way I have been. It seems like a small price to pay to have something to look forward to, even if, in the day-to-day, this trip seems untethered to any reality I can foresee.

I once went to a museum exhibit about Einstein, and the only idea I took away from it was that movement stretches time. I don't recall the science behind this, something to do with curvature I think. What I was left with was the understanding that the more you moved, the longer your life felt. Whether it was actually longer, I'm not sure. But every time I am behind an elderly person creeping up Broadway, or lurching their way around Zabar's, I think of this—this determination to keep moving—and resolve to stretch more. But how does one mark time without movement or signposts? It remains flat, endless, and meaningless all at once. And so, as the weather warms and the city unfurls, the trip hovers just off to the side of my vision, a nice idea. It reminds me of lists we were asked to make as children, declaring what we wanted to be when we grew up. The last time I saw him in person, my youngest nephew told me he wanted to be a skyscraper. Over breakfast, I'd been reading him a picture book about New York, and as he spooned up his cereal, gazing at the illustrated pages of towering buildings, this struck him as the thing to be. This trip feels similar: the thing to be, and impossible at the same time.

In New York, as predicted, the new roaring twenties arrive right on schedule. Starting in mid-June, when the first round of vaccines begin to take effect, an orgy-like atmosphere rolls across the city. It feels like the collision of any number of events, and decades: Mardi Gras slamming into late-nineties New York summer. In the parks people wear as little as possible of anything they can get their hands on. Cutoffs of all shapes and sizes. Tops ripped and tied on at strange angles. Skin oozing out from midriffs and thighs. Cleavages bursting. Crotches bulging. The parks are overlaid with picnic blankets, the corners overlapping one another, food from one spilled onto the other. One afternoon I walk through Tompkins Square and am handed slices of cake from strangers. I'm invited to join groups. No one can get enough of one another. Pulling one's mask up from below the chin to cover one's face when passing a person in close proximity on the sidewalk becomes the new tipping of the hat. I see you, it says. Thank god, I see you. And I care about you.

It is short-lived. By the end of July, as I'm packing for my flight, new variants have rolled in and the city is resignedly moving to the early stages of another, if not collapse, then shutdown. Like closing up a summer house ahead of a typhoon. New York begins to batten down.

So far the borders are remaining open, at least in the direction I'm traveling, but a familiar sense of foreboding attaches itself to everything I do in preparation for the trip. I feel like I'm moving in a thick fog. I can't see too far ahead, so anything but contained, carefully considered movement will be injurious in some way. Even though the pitfalls ahead are not yet visible, I assume their presence, from big to small: The flight will be delayed. Customs will be clogged. My vaccination card won't be accepted. The man I'm renting from will get sick and have to stay in Paris. I will get stuck somewhere I can't afford, which truth be told, is basically everywhere, and I won't be able to leave. These are just some of the items on an endless list in my head titled "Things That Can and Probably Will Go Wrong."

And yet, the perceived risk of jetting away, only slightly ahead of a new virus wave, is, in my mind, only incrementally greater than any other decision I make. My life as a single forty-six-year-old writer—outside of marriage, outside of motherhood, outside of payroll, outside of ritual, outside of, for the past year anyway, real-life human contact—is a life lived largely without a safety net. I am my own fallback. I play all the roles. I'm the person who thinks five steps ahead down all the paths, envisions the various outcomes, and then role-plays all the people I will have to be to solve it. Whether it is risky to get on a plane pales in comparison to what could potentially be more of this . . . not just isolation, but stagnancy. Total invisibility. Paralysis. Leaving feels less like a risk than a necessity.

TWO

Good Decisions

What no one prepares you for as a woman is for everything to go right. When you are a woman alone, this is never even suggested as a possibility. I will know fellow women who travel solo by their rapt attention when I recount what follows with a level of detail that would exhaust a person accustomed to, for better or worse, traveling with a companion. It's the solo lady version of parents telling one another they've successfully sleep-trained their child or managed to introduce a vegetable into their diet. Similarly, I will watch these women's faces light up in a combination of recognition, voyeurism, and relief at seeing an ideal version of their life out in the world.

Here's what happens:

The flight is not canceled. The borders are not closed. I am not sick. Neither is the man I'm renting from, who is already in the air on the way to New York to see his family by the time I depart.

There is no traffic. I make it to JFK, a distance of fourteen miles, in twenty-five minutes, which is forty-five minutes less than the usual time it takes to get there.

There is no line at security.

The plane takes off on time.

Not only that, it's half empty. There is no one behind me, or beside me; my economy aisle seat in the middle row becomes a bed I can stretch out on.

Shortly after we reach cruising altitude, the pilot comes on to let us know we have a strong tailwind and will be arriving nearly an hour early. "It looks like we'll even have a gate waiting for us." He has the sort of gruff male voice that immediately brings me comfort because it makes me feel like we are being flown by a person who has trained in some sort of Top Gun school and, given the opportunity, will refer to turbulence as "chop." Recent years spent dissecting how we've internalized the lethal legacy of the patriarchy does not keep me from being made to feel safe by this.

I feel strangely connected to the other passengers on the plane, as if we are all making this leap together. As though we are a select group who has decided that, after all, life is for the living, or at least the leaping. This feeling of triumph recedes as thoughts of the people not on this plane roll in—the people I am leaving behind, so many of whom remain tethered, by money, by family, by job, by children. I am untethered. Or if not exactly that, then my tethers have the capacity to unfurl at great lengths without ever breaking. I can be simultaneously connected and disconnected. And now here we are, the fortunate adventurers, hurtling into the air. It's the most motion I have experienced in more than a year. I could never have conceived of a world in which I'd describe flying as enjoyable, and yet, right now I can't think of a single thing that would bring me more pleasure than this sense of velocity currently racing through my body.

As the earth and the lights of New York City drop away beneath us, my brain clears, my thoughts sharpen. I leave behind the person I have been for the last eighteen months—reliable, solitary—like a snake shedding its skin. I feel as though I could look out the window and see that former shell of myself below, there at her desk on the seventeenth floor, a little hollow, very transparent. A ghost of months past. But I don't look back. Instead, I lean back in my seat and reappear to myself as a person in motion. I like what I see. Then I fall asleep.

When I wake, there is clean morning sunlight shining through open windows and the flight attendants are serving breakfast. Do I want a *chocolat chaud?*

I am away.

And still the good fortune continues! At Charles de Gaulle there is indeed a gate waiting for us. There is no line at customs. The French agent scans my vaccination card, stamps my passport, and *smiles,* wishing me a good day. My suitcase is waiting for me at the luggage carousel. The RER is in the station when I come down. One minute after I board it departs and we make it all the way to Châtelet without stalling.

I am stunned by all of this. I feel as if the world has taken me by the hand. Thrown open a door. Raised a glass and toasted my good decision-making. Really, when was the last time anyone has smoothly departed from New York to *anywhere?* When was the last time some-one smoothly arrived in Paris? Has it ever happened? Was I possibly the first to experience this phenomenon?

And yet, here I am making my way up an unusually quiet Rue de la Roquette barely nine hours after walking out my front door. *Nine hours.*

A message pops up on my WhatsApp just as the church that marks my street comes into view. It's the British woman on the second floor from whom I'm picking up the keys.

"Hello again. Just to remind you the street code is 6734. You take a right at the letter boxes and you will see a glass door leading to a staircase . . ."

This *is* new. There hadn't been a second door there last time. Per-haps this was why the key had been left with her instead of just under the doormat. The message continues:

"You press on the arrows to find my name and then you press the bell to ring me and I shall answer and let you in. Second floor right-hand door."

This degree of explanation makes me think she must be older. No one under sixty feels the need to hand-hold through text like this. I'm briefly reminded of my mother. I have been perversely grateful every day since March 2020 that she died before the pandemic and we didn't have to spend this time worried about her well-being in a locked-down nursing home. Somewhere in my desk at home sits an old phone on which I am still able to access all her voicemails to me. Each one begins the same way: "Oh hi, sweetie, it's Mom," as if I might not rec-ognize her voice. I try to picture my mother navigating texting; by the time cell phones were common, she was too sick to understand how to use them. I imagine that, were she still alive, she would approach it as she did a letter, formally and at length, writing out in detail everything she wanted to say, complete with salutation, perfect grammar, and complimentary close. I think of her beautiful handwriting—everyone remarked on it—and how, until recently, pen to paper was some small extension of how we each operated in the world. All these unique parts of ourselves have been lost to the two dimensions of screens.

The front door code to the building is the same as it ever was; my fingers fly over the numbers as though I had just been here last week. Inside, the spacious entry is cool and dark. There is a second doorway, and I am buzzed up without conversation. Up the shallow curved staircase, the suitcase and I now make our way, one slow step at a time; I'm sweating, real sweat, not just perspiration, and I pause on each landing to catch my breath and switch hands.

I used to be an excellent packer, shrewd and discerning; I could travel on the contents of a carry-on for weeks. But when I was laying out the items to take on this trip, it occurred to me that I no longer understood myself as a person in the world. I couldn't envision myself out there, in it, doing things. Who would I be when I left this apartment? What does that person wear and where do they go? I had no answer for this, so instead of settling on a few items and leaving space for what I might find out there, I packed all the versions of me. And now I am carting them all up many flights of stairs and they are very heavy.

The British woman with the key is on the second floor, which is the third floor for me; the French count the ground floor as zero. It's quiet on the stairs; the only noise comes from the courtyard, through the windows that have been cut into the wall halfway between each landing. I can hear recycling and garbage bins being opened and slammed shut as the bistro on the ground floor warms up to the day. The sweat begins to dribble down my face.

Sometimes in moments like this, when managing my own life feels quite literally too heavy and unwieldy, I imagine what it might be like to have help. I imagine there being another person beside me with whom I could think through some of these details. Who could go upstairs and get the key, for instance, and then return and shoulder part of the weight of the bags. Who could say, We're almost there. Or just laugh with me at the ridiculousness of this. Who could release me, even briefly, from being all the people I need to be. Who could make things just a bit *easier*.

This shadowy figure, however, is absent today even from the furthest reaches of my own imagination. In the past year, when I did manage to emerge and see friends it was usually for distanced walks around Central Park. They all had the real-life version of that other person I was sometimes tempted to imagine. That theoretical built-in support. And yet here they always were, with me. Round the park we'd go, in some reversed, pandemic, domestic version of *The Things They Carried*, as they unloaded about how much they resented their spouses, their work, their suffocating apartments. How utterly overwhelmed they were. Are still. How they were staggering under weights and responsibilities, too heavy for anyone to shoulder alone, even while being suffocated by the presence of others who, in theory anyway, were supposed to make things better. Their partners were useless. Below contempt. "I loathe my children," they'd say to me in a whisper, despite the fact there was no one around, as though they were confessing to an unimaginable crime. "I hate them. Hate," they'd say again, as if sensing skepticism in my silence. *Why* had they made the decisions they'd made? Each time, I'd wait until they were done, had caught their breath, and then I'd firmly let them know they were the third person to tell me this, this week. The fifth this month. That it felt like nearly everyone I knew currently wanted a divorce. To be alone. To have made different decisions. That they were not alone in what they were experiencing.

Then I'd return home to my little apartment, actually alone, having let them unburden free of judgment (perhaps the greatest gift one can give), having helped them shoulder the weight of their lives, and I'd have to try to figure out how to do the same for myself. How was I supposed to shoulder myself? That is what this trip is. Me making myself feel better.

I reach the second floor, sweat now fully streaming down my face, arms burning. But inside I am aflame with gratitude that I have only myself to carry around, however heavy all these me's might currently be.

I wipe my face and catch my breath before I press the buzzer. The door opens six inches. The woman who emerges is a little stooped—the way thin women get when they don't do yoga as they age—and graying. This is all I can make out. Her face is covered by a mask, her hands gloved. The light in this corner of the hallway is dim. The keys I am here to pick up shoot out through the narrow opening.

The caution she exudes pushes me back a step. It feels like both an admonishment and a jarring reality check. You are being reckless, it says.

"You're early," is what she actually says. It's an observation, not an accusation.

"Yes, well . . ." I begin to explain about the tailwinds, and customs, and the RER, excited to have someone to share it with, but she is already retreating as though pulled by an invisible cord attached to her spine. "WhatsApp me if you have any questions," she says.

The tone is friendly, but the door is shut and locked before I can respond and explain that I actually know Paris reasonably well. That I've spent every August here for the last five years. Except for last year, of course. I stare at the closed door; her cautiousness creeps around the edges of my lighthearted mind-set, but instead of dimming it, it makes it appear even brighter and stranger. Perhaps it's just the thrill of being reacted to by a stranger.

I continue my climb. Three more *étages* and I can kick this suitcase to the corner and attempt to transform into what I prefer to be seen as, at all times and everywhere: a local.

Finally, the door. I slide the thick key in and hear the long iron bar slide down, once, and again. And then . . .

I'm immediately dropped into a time capsule. Nothing has changed. It's as though someone sealed the apartment up shortly after I left two years ago, and now I'm the first to return. You hear of those apartments in Paris sometimes. Ones that have been sealed since the war. Everything left, just *as is*. Like an Egyptian burial tomb, but less intentional. I'm having a similar experience. There is the same white wobbly table leaning against the built-in bookshelves. The same pillows with the mirrored squares sewn on, piled on the denim-covered couch that looks like a futon but doesn't pull out. There are the same books lined up on the shelves in the same order, and the tangle of power cords and adapters in the far corner. Nearest me on the bookshelf I see the same metal plate of foreign coins, now under a layer of dust.

I've sometimes found it difficult to mark the passage of time in my own life. Being untethered, thrilling though it often is, also means being unstuck in time for much of the time. I'm disconnected from nearly every ritual commonly used to mark progress and worthiness: engagement parties, weddings, baby showers, children's birthdays, children's school years, marriage anniversaries, Mother's Day. After a certain age, celebrating your own birthday can feel like an exercise in mustering the resolve to provide a narrative around it that does not involve apology, shame, ruefulness, or defiance. Anything but the word *fabulous.* I've ceased to feel any of these things about my age, but continually being asked to find the language to articulate how I *do* feel— and the truth is, I feel great, most of the time, but even this declaration inevitably takes on a defensive, middle-finger quality—is not work I'm interested in doing for free. The result is I'm sometimes left with the sensation that time is sliding away. My life a flat line. It's easy for me to forget how old I am. Not in the sense of maturity. But literally. I sometimes have to do the math.

There is also the matter of my own increasingly unreliable body. From age fourteen to forty it operated with military punctuality; you could have set a watch by the time my uterus kept. No longer. My body has detached itself from its own timeline. On more than a few occasions in the last year I've been compelled to ask the question: Virus or perimenopause? (In the winter months this shifts to: Virus, perimenopause, or my century-old radiator?) My doctor, while wonderful, has no answers. "You're getting to that age" has become the most frequently repeated sentence in my appointments with her. When I press and ask, "Is this normal?" she says, "No one is sure," because "no one" has ever done the research into the universal experience of half the population. But this might soon change, she assures me after she asks if I've scheduled my appointment for the newly released vaccine, which took only a year to create. "Your generation is accustomed to having information," she tells me. "You're all furious there is none." When she says this, I *am* furious, but it doesn't last. I can be angry about only so many things at the same time. And even then, I'm not very good at it.

Increasingly, I experience time as one of those old flip-books that you have to thumb through quickly to animate the illustration: time can whip by and I can feel as though I've only taken a few steps. The stasis of this apartment underscores the jarring sensation that after I left here, almost exactly two years ago, I somehow ceased to exist. That the intervening months have been swallowed into some sort of black hole during which no progress was made, no development, no transformation. And that any transformation I may have undergone has had very little to do with my own day-to-day experience and very much to do with witnessing so many other people experience isolation and uncertainty for the first time, and violently balk at the realities of it. If anything, the last year and a half has bizarrely felt like a collective, if unintentional, pat on the back. A *Wow, it really is hard to be alone.* To not live a life that provides a five-year plan. To fend for yourself with little to no security net. The world disappearing from view at times has had the effect of suddenly making me feel extremely seen.

But now, standing here in the doorway of this unchanged space— which, were it to appear on a rental app, could reasonably be described as a quaint, classic, Parisian flat—what the identical backdrop suddenly allows me to see are past versions of myself at that table. The me who arrived here with a book deal five years ago, terrified of the task before me. The one who came in the aftermath of my mother's death. The paradox of all time-travel stories: What happens to us if, when we leave our own timeline, we slam into another version of ourselves? Does the universe implode? Is history irrevocably altered? But lately when I encounter past versions of myself, all I feel is sympathy and admiration. Good job, kid, I want to say. You did your best. Keep going.

I pull back the dark drapes and swing the tall windows all the way out. The smells from the street slide into the apartment. Onions. Garlic. Butter. A preview of French lunches being prepped. There is no breakfast in Paris. You can find a few brunches if you want, but the breakfast hour, the diner, the 6:00 a.m. coffee cart that launches New York into its day, does not really exist here. From past experience, I know that by the time it's time for me to fly home, this will be the thing I crave most. An 8:00 a.m. omelet with greasy hash browns. An egg sandwich from the deli. A large bodega coffee, sweet and white.

From my vantage at the open window, I can hear the thump of music. There are no air conditioners here. In the summer months you live with the noise of your own life and the lives of everyone else—sneezes, sex, cigarettes, phone calls, yelling. "In Paris we fight and fuck together," my friend Nina likes to say.

Standing at the window, it's hard for me to tell if the music is coming from the corner or from below. The sound bounces off the buildings and down the narrow streets, making it difficult to trace. In another week these places will shutter up for the remainder of the month. *En Vacances.* I wonder if empty Paris will have the same mesmerizing effect it's had in the past after so much emptiness. If the sense of being granted a rare gift, the illusion of ownership, will persist.

The bells of the church begin to ring. I count them. It's 9:00 a.m. The first Monday of August. I am in Paris.

THREE

Prized Control, Yearned
After Momentum

'm overcome with a sense of wonder. If I had to turn around right
now and go home, I would still be satisfied with this brief excur-
sion. I came, I saw, I touched. It's still here.

But I don't have to leave.

Instead, I drag the monstrosity containing all the me's into the
bedroom and throw it open.

Now that I can take in its contents, my suitcase strikes me as extremely reasonable.

I've brought five vintage caftans; two dresses; two jumpsuits, one
of which is vintage; six T-shirts; three tank tops; four blouses; three
pairs of pants; three black leggings; two pairs of jeans; two long-sleeved
shirts; one sweater; a vintage Issey Miyake wind coat in camel; a
proper raincoat in leopard that I bought at Merci two years ago when
I got caught in a rainstorm; a black blazer from H&M that is the
exact one Natasha Lyonne wears in *Russian Doll*; two silk scarves; one

cashmere scarf; my running clothes; three swimsuits, one the closest approximation I could find to the one Romy Schneider wears in *La Piscine*, which I'd seen six times at Film Forum before leaving New York. In the insert are fifteen pairs of underwear, unnecessary as there is a washing machine in the apartment; five pairs of socks; my yoga shorts and tank top; and a trucker cap in camouflage with the word *JAWS* written in silver lettering across it.

In *The White Album*, Joan Didion famously wrote down her packing list, radical at the time—Tampax!—and revealing in its intimacy and simplicity. As a storytelling device, it was admirable in what it told the reader about the writer, about her life, and about what it meant to be a woman in the world, without seeming to say much.

Didion wrote the list in 1979, but it has gained new life in the last ten years, surpassing, at times, the popularity of her "Goodbye to All That" essay about leaving New York, which has seemingly been re-done by every writer leaving the city ever since. Less mentioned is the fact she returned twenty-five years later and made it her permanent home. (Does any other city require a defense of departure? Did people feel the need to declare why they were leaving Paris? Was it that New York was an identity and other cities were just places to live, or does New York simply attract a higher concentration of narcissists?)

Didion's packing list, however, is perfectly suited to our social media times, which strives to reduce all life to small performances of intimacy. And at the same time add credence to the daily activities of women. There is a similar vibe in Nora Ephron's essay "On Maintenance," from the collection *I Feel Bad About My Neck*. In it, Ephron writes at length about upkeep: "There's a reason why forty, fifty, and sixty don't look the way they used to, and it's not because of feminism, or better living through exercise. It's because of hair dye." Between Ephron and Didion (who were apparently friends for half a century— I would have liked an invite to that dinner party), an entire corner of the internet finds its source. Whenever someone needs a reliable traffic generator for their website or follow count, they can turn to Didion's list and lean on her "bag with: shampoo, toothbrush and paste, Basis soap, razor, deodorant, aspirin, prescriptions, Tampax, face cream, powder, baby oil." So easy. So succinct! So serious. So worthy. It gives gravitas to minutiae. So much of women's lives are considered minutiae, the appeal in this sense is understandable.

But if you go back and read the full essay, it goes beyond the list. Didion spends the following three hundred–odd words or so *telling* the reader what to notice. "Notice the deliberate anonymity," she says. "Notice the mohair throw . . . for the motel room in which the air conditioning could not be turned off. . . . Notice the typewriter for the airport." She wanted the reader to understand that that this was a list "made by someone who prized control, yearned after momentum, . . . determined to play her role as if she had the script, heard her cues, knew the narrative."

Needless to say, judging by the explosion of clothes I have just sorted, I have none of these things. No script. No role.

Before we'd all been sent inside, I'd been in rooms with professionals, all women, who were extremely excited by the idea of adapting a memoir I'd written about turning forty, without children or a partner, for the screen. They'd read it and seen themselves in it— sometimes for the first time—and were thrilled. At times, a note of possessiveness crept in. As if I'd nailed the details so correctly, it felt as if I were telling *their* story. Which I came to realize was just one of the dangers of having so few stories about women outside the narrow ones our culture celebrates about marriage and motherhood—the perverse comfort it can bring by allowing you to think you are *unique*. When in fact, the uniqueness, if it can be called that, was simply in the telling, not the living. (And so much of the ability to tell was a function of where I lived, and who I knew, and, to paraphrase another internet favorite, the dresses I wore and where I went and what I did in them.)

The trick to getting this all on the screen was figuring out what the narrative was. "What is the problem she is trying to solve?" I was asked over and over. "What is the story?" "The narrative," I would say, "is that there is no narrative." "The story," I would say, "is figuring out how to live when there was no role you could determine to play, or script to follow, or cues to hear." You are all the dresses, and none.

This was an insurmountable problem in the end. At least for me. It's possible a better, more seasoned television writer could have sorted it out. But I was left with the impression that the only female problems we understood women to have, and subsequently know how to solve, were love and children. Repeat. No one could figure out how to put another problem on the screen, because what other problem could there really be? What exactly was our heroine supposed to be working toward? Eve Babitz wrote that women are not prepared to have everything, "not when the 'everything' isn't about living happily ever after with the prince (where even if it falls through and the prince runs away with the baby-sitter, there's at least a *precedent*)."

We tried lots of different ideas: The inciting incident was that our heroine lost her job, but then what? She got another one? So what.

The inciting incident was that her boyfriend broke up with her and she had to figure out how to live alone. But then what? The inciting incident was that her rent was doubled, but then she moved in with her oldest friend in New York and her family (this is a true story), but then what? In a moment of true desperation, we tried to make her a worker in an Amazon depot in the middle of the country. But then what? How were we supposed to know she was *okay*. That she was *successful*.

After the book came out, I would hear from some readers who wanted to know if I thought I was the first woman who had not been married or not had children. Which, lol (the only appropriate answer to that question is, truly, lol). They all seemed to have a happy aunt in the attic they wanted me to know about. Point me to the movie, the book, the show that depicts this, I wanted to say (but didn't; at the very least, years on the internet had taught me the art of the nonresponse). The only example *I* could think of (and possibly because of this, the one I refer to in so much of what I write) was the film *An Unmarried Woman*, starring Jill Clayburgh. In it, Clayburgh, who was thirty-three years old during filming, plays an—I think we are supposed to understand her as middle-aged—educated, presumably happily married woman who has a teenage daughter (sixteen or seventeen) and lives on a high floor on the East Sixties, with an extraordinary view of Second Avenue stretching all the way downtown. During the day she works at an art gallery on West Broadway in pre–Dean & DeLuca SoHo. One day her husband meets her for lunch and tells her he's fallen in love and is leaving her for a younger woman. The rest of the film is about her falling apart and then putting her life back together. Including a passionate love affair with a bearded, tempestuous

I'M MOSTLY HERE TO ENJOY MYSELF

artist. When her husband comes begging for her back, she turns him away. She also spurns the artist's offer for her to come live with him upstate. Instead, she decamps, by herself (her daughter is off to college), to a Brooklyn brownstone with a bay window and a backyard (I think—this movie is not available to stream anywhere so I must go off memory). The final shot is of her weaving her way up West Broadway trying to navigate her way while holding a huge painting given to her by her artist lover. It looks like a great sail on a ship she barely has control over as she sets out on her unmarried woman odyssey. *Tell me the story of a complicated woman.*

After some extensive lockdown googling, I sourced the painter—Paul Jenkins—and the title of the actual painting—*Phenomena Rain Palace*—and then found a copy of it online. It sits framed in my apartment directly across from the original theater card for *An Unmarried Woman* that I subsequently tracked down on eBay, which depicts Clayburgh leaping about in her underwear. I slid this card over an original poster for *Lolita* given to me by a friend who left New York for Los Angeles years ago and couldn't manage the heavy gilt frame in her luggage.

In the end there was no TV show. It's easier to write divorce and widowhood it turns out. Only young women, with plenty of runway ahead to come to their senses, get to have messy challenges.

I close the suitcase and look around, still amazed it was all so heavy. Unpacked, it really doesn't look like that much, let alone too much. It certainly doesn't look like the weight of another body. It looks like the closet of a person with a full life. "Dress for the life you want" is a quote I also attribute to Diana Vreeland, though it sounds too basic for *D.V.* and is likely just something I read on Instagram. To me, all these now unpacked items simply say that I am ready for any-thing. To be anyone. How this will be accomplished is less clear to me. I've only thought as far ahead as getting here.

Finally, I unpack the books from the reusable shopping bag I've wrapped them in. I've brought Barbara Tuchman's *A Distant Mirror* with me, her history of the bubonic plague, known as the Black Death, with the intention of getting a sense of what we might expect in the coming years. In the opening pages she states she has *not* chosen a woman through which to tell the story because "any medieval woman whose life was adequately documented would be atypical." (The choice "is thus narrowed to a male member of the Second Estate.") I put it on the small metal desk that sits beside the bed, along with a copy of *Save the Cat!*, a popular guide on how to write a novel. The author posits that there are fifteen plot points or "beats" every successful story follows, such as the "Inciting Incident," the "Midpoint," or "All Is Lost." The author also argues that every book ever written fits into ten genres.

Which am I, right now, I wonder. Am I currently engaged in a "Rite of Passage"? ("A hero must endure pain and torment brought about by life's common challenges.") A "Fool Triumphant"? ("An underesti-mated, underdog hero is pitted against some kind of 'establishment.'") Maybe I'm in search of the "Golden Fleece." ("A hero [or group] goes on a 'road trip' of some type [even if there's no actual road] in search of one thing.") What if I'm experiencing all these genres simultane-ously? What if the story I'm in is about living without a recognizable story? Are there beats for that?

My only challenge right now is exhaustion. Fortunately, the solu-tion is directly in front of me: the bed. I've solved my first problem, overcome my inciting incident: I've arrived. I can be horizontal again.

The truth is, I should stay up. I should ride out the day and get on a Paris schedule. I should not risk the insomnia that will take hold if I'm careless with my jet lag. Instead, I plunge into sleep. The kind you only get as an adult when you are jet-lagged. When I wake it's 5:00 p.m. The music outside has disappeared and been replaced by the clink of silverware and glasses. On my phone are a series of Whats-App messages from Nina.

"Sancerre. 6:00 p.m."

FOUR

Fruitz

Over the years, I've created an entire circle of friends in Paris. I sometimes joke that they are the Paris chapter of a secret international group of unmarried women whom I seem to gather to me everywhere I travel. And they are waiting for me here now at Sancerre: Nina, Aarti, and Sandra (with her little dog, Marcel). With them also is a younger blonde woman, wearing a short flowery dress that shows off her long legs. "I'm Ellie," she says in a crisp British accent. When I first arrive, all our greetings are amusingly muted, as though we were just here last week. The calm, familiar tone belies the constant text messages we've exchanged over the last weeks and months or during our lengthy weekly Zooms. The multiple exclamation points, the repeated assertions that *"I can't wait!!"* It also underscores the sense that time has somehow looped back on itself and we were all only just here. Perhaps just yesterday, having this same drink together.

We are sitting outside in the 3rd arrondissement across from the Square du Temple Elie Wiesel, a green jewel of a *parc* that has a pond and a playground and sweeping green trees. The sun is setting and the light is diffusing over Paris, casting everything in a pink and gold glow. I'm told the grand apartments lining the square, with their grandiose moldings depicting heavenly creatures aloft, never go on the market. They simply stay in the family for decades, more than a century in some cases. The square is usually packed and lively with sounds of children and music, but even here, in the heart of the Marais, things are quiet. Or at least muted.

On the table are the last flakes of the fries that have just been demolished. A *planche*, with both cheese and charcuterie, has just been ordered. It arrives on a wooden board, piled high with sliced prosciutto, rounds of salami, a mountain of sliced baguette, and *chèvre* so gooey it oozes into the squares of foil-wrapped butter—bread is never served here without butter, no matter that the bread in front of us is for the cheese and meats.

I stumble through an order of rosé. It will be days before what little French I have catches up with me. By week two, I'll be able to get through a drink and *boulangerie* order without the person I'm speaking to immediately switching to English. But not yet. I can barely remember the word for glass (*verre*). Nina simply repeats my order for me. Somehow this discomfort with language only serves to highlight that I am now with people with whom I speak a common tongue. I don't mean English, though we all do speak that.

On the surface we are a bit of a motley crew. Arriving here from divergent paths. Nina was my first Paris friend. We were set up on a blind friend date by a mutual acquaintance five years ago at the end of my first full August in Paris. I was here trying to finish the first draft of my memoir, and she was here for a weekslong holiday following the finalization of a tough divorce from an American man she'd met at twenty-three and married not long after. Nina is from Finland but moved to Los Angeles following her marriage and had been there ever since. We have both been through the American media mines, her on the West Coast in entertainment journalism and me in New York, and that proved a common enough base to build on at first. But from there sprung a full-fledged friendship, a shared sense of fun and understanding of how we wanted to live in the world. A few months after returning to Los Angeles, she rented an apartment in Paris, and a year after that she was able to buy a small one-bedroom in the 11th. I sometimes call her Timotei because her long, silky blonde hair reminds me of the shampoo commercials that played constantly during my childhood, which featured lithe blonde women brushing their platinum hair peacefully by a waterfall. During lockdown, she met a kind, quiet American living in Helsinki on Tinder and a year later the long-distance relationship they have constructed is still going strong.

Nina is my baseline here. The foundation on which so many other relationships were built. It was through her I met Sandra, also a journalist, the following summer. Sandra is from California. She won't tell any of us her exact age. She looks like Snow White. Pale skin, black hair, red lips. She is perfectly turned out every time she leaves the house. Where I might stumble to the corner in leggings, I've never seen her not exquisitely accessorized. Bangles. Impeccably tied neck scarves. Sandra is a person who can pull off capes. Without fail, every time I see her, I ask about some part of the outfit she's wearing. Is it vintage Celine? YSL? And every time she tells me it's Zara. Or

J.Crew. Both inevitably purchased secondhand. It's a particular person who can make mass-produced clothes look like couture. But she does.

For decades Sandra has been a highly accomplished reporter for major entertainment magazines. When she moved to Paris she lived the media dream, becoming the Paris correspondent, attending festivals, profiling celebrities. She was on the career trajectory to become editor in chief of something impressive. And then the media world fell apart, like an old Wile E. Coyote cartoon where the tracks lead up and up and then somehow disappear. Goodbye to all that. Six months ago, she was laid off from her high-level reporting job and is currently paying the bills writing captions for a shoe company's Instagram account. "At least it pays well," she says with a shrug.

Over the years, I've come to believe Sandra knows everything. And has been almost everywhere. Once I told her how an Instagram account run by a sanctuary for orphaned elephants in Kenya was my lockdown happy place. "I went there," she said matter-of-factly. "You can see the elephants at feeding time, but it's crowded." She once hired a machine gun–carrying taxi driver and did an overnight climb of a mountain near the Somalia border. "That's incredible," I told her, imagining some sort of *Out of Africa* life-altering vastness. Another shrug: "At the top of the mountain you can see the highway being built by the Chinese. All the highways are being built by the Chinese. This is part of the Belt and Road Initiative to more easily export natural resources to China, and quite controversial because of the debt load, political maneuvering, and resulting influence. It's a huge foreign policy issue at the moment." This is often how our conversations go. She thinks donating clothes is useless altruism: "I've been to the ports in Africa. It just comes in in huge containers and gets thrown away and contributes to the waste." She operates with a level of realism bordering on cynicism that I assume is a result of all this knowledge, but also will only listen to K-pop. Everyone loves K-pop these days, but Sandra has been telling me about it for years now. One summer, curious about this art form that had such a grip on her, I attended a K-pop show with her at the Bataclan—she camped out overnight and got a spot in the front row. I showed up ten minutes beforehand and stood at the back, mesmerized by all the screaming but not quite understanding. She will send Nina and me updates on the lives of BTS members. I'm forever a disappointment to her for not watching the K-drama *Romance Is a Bonus Book*.

Nina and Sandra and I share a gallows humor that never fails to bring me joy. During lockdown it was a lifeline. We've had plenty of nights of dancing, and drinking, and eating, but in the end it's our shared sense of the impending apocalypse as a source of comfort that often proves most enjoyable. On our weekly Zooms these past long months we'd plan our lives in the tunnels under Helsinki. How would we get there? Who would be responsible for bringing what? How would Marcel cope? I can be my darkest self with them and know that we will turn it into a recurring punch line. The directness and realism are, to me anyway, some of the great attributes of friendship at this age and speak to an enormous level of trust we have in one another's best intentions. And also, we are never not laughing.

Aarti is from India. Pretty and sweet faced, she's a decade younger than me but could easily pass for someone in their twenties. She likes to joke that even though she speaks five languages they are useless to her in her life here because outside of India, where there are twenty-two official languages, no one else speaks them. Aarti was recruited to Paris five years ago to do an important job that I don't fully understand. She hasn't been able to return to India since 2020 and has no clear idea of when that might change. I sometimes think that Aarti has, by any measure, not just the measure of miles, traveled the greatest distance to get here. She is the middle child and the second daughter of traditional Indian parents. To move to Paris, live on her own, date a non-Indian man, let alone live with him, to have no intention of marrying, and less to have children, has required her to travel so far from where she was expected to be. I marvel that we find ourselves in the same place. I once asked her if her parents were proud of her. She laughed. "Of course not; I'm always a disappointment to them."

I feel like while all I had to do to get here was buy a plane ticket and walk to the corner, Aarti had to run ten marathons, carrying the weight of all the cultural and familial disappointment, to get to the same place. But here we are.

What I share with the women at this table is the common language of not being married and not having children. It is an enormous relief to not have to translate my life. Or feel like I am reporting from a foreign country, editing my story accordingly. When I'm with these women, I don't have to refrain from mentioning the hours I'm able to devote to reading, or the trips I'm able to take, simply to avoid being told I'm lucky. I'm not required to make empathizing one-sided conversations about the toddler who will eat only one color of food (thanks to the vast time spread of my friends' pregnancies, I have been having the toddler conversation for the better part of fifteen years). Here I can complain about the inability to get a mortgage without some sort of outside financial help without becoming an object of pity. Here all our conversations are underpinned with the understanding that things can be great and hard at the same time. At this table, we've all made the same choices; we're all secure in them. As a starting line it is an extraordinary gift, and I have missed it.

Even without the pandemic it's been a strange decade. As I move through my forties, I've found myself becoming increasingly offensive to a certain woman. She is usually ten to twenty years older than me, though not always; comfortably wealthy; deep into a marriage; with children who are grown or close to being so. She is always white. Always. On paper she embodies an ideal that makes me suspect she feels most satisfied when she's filling out forms and checking off the boxes. She almost never likes me. Which stands out because, frankly, I'm accustomed to being liked. Her aversion to me emits like a scent, and I catch it the way I imagine animals do. The more fully I occupy my own life, the stronger that scent gets. I've come to suspect I'm some sort of proof. Proof, perhaps, that a *New York Times* wedding announcement does not shore up matters of life the way one was convinced it might? Though this feels too simplistic. What really irks this woman, I've come to realize, is that I appear to be enjoying myself. I have veered off the narrow path laid out for women to be successful in the world, and it turns out I'm fine. Sometimes better, sometimes worse, but mostly fine. Which inevitably throws a question mark at the end of her decisions. I mentioned this to Nina once, and she understood immediately: "We're an attack on the value system of certain people." As if my, or our, enjoyment undermines the hard work they have devoted to staying the path. And worse, calls into question the rewards that path offers. If I don't feel bad about my life, how can they feel good? I used to feel the need to launch a rousing defense of myself in the face of this, but that's gone away. It feels like enough that my life is no longer a question mark to me. Here at this table, I don't need to answer for myself.

Maybe because we've been in such constant contact, no catch-up is necessary. I have declared my desire for desire, and we are already plotting how best to make this happen. The *planche* has barely arrived before we plunge into a discussion on dating apps. What do people use in Paris now? I'm eager to know. A few years ago, it was an app called Happn, which matches you with people you "happen" to be within a certain distance of; maybe they live next door, maybe they are simply walking by your apartment when you log on. But it has gone out of fashion, presumably because no one was moving around enough in the last year to make it interesting. Tinder is stale. Bumble feels like a lot of work. Did I know about Fruitz?

Ellie discovered Fruitz during lockdown. Lockdown in Paris was both more extreme and more rational than in New York. In Paris, citizens maintained their universal health care and immediately began receiving regular payments from the government regardless of their employment status. In turn they were allowed outside for only an hour every day, within a circumscribed distance from their apartment. If they needed to venture outside the approved radius, they needed a permission slip, which they were required to write and time-stamp for themselves. The Parisian parks were all locked (in normal times this happens at dusk).

In New York, there was no money, save a one-time payment, unless you were eligible for unemployment. Millions lost their employment-based health care, and nothing was locked. The parks were open and empty. Signs posted at the New York City subway entrances read:

STOP. ARE YOU AN ESSENTIAL WORKER? NO? WHY ARE YOU HERE? GO HOME.
People simply stayed inside out of fear, unless they had to work, and others fled from the city like rats from a sinking ship.

During one of the pandemic waves, Ellie, alone in her flat outside the Périph, had matched on Fruitz with a man who owned a restaurant. She'd slipped out against curfew and slid through the dark streets. When she arrived, she discovered her date had opened the entire restaurant for her and made her a five-course dinner. So romantic, I say. I ask if they are still seeing each other. She shrugs, no.

Ellie is still a blank slate to me. All I know so far, beyond this dating story, is that she is fluent in five languages, including French, and works here as a translator. She's tall and blonde and, even though she's British, she could easily pass for a French Instagram girl. The forthrightness with which she tells her story is appealing. The older I get the less I find I stand on ceremony. My conversations with other women almost immediately just get to the point. I don't think twice about talking about health, body issues, sex, insecurity. The pretense of . . . I suppose it's shame, has evaporated. The directness of expressing how I exist in the world becomes a life force. Encountering people who are not put off by this, who do the same, is immediately comforting and intensely enjoyable.

Of course, I know people in New York who online dated during lockdown. Who got on video chats and then committed to strict quarantines before finally meeting in person. I did not. I chose the city instead. The one upside of being on my own was that I could leave the apartment each day without exposing anyone. Round and round the empty city I went, on foot, and on my bike, taking it all in, trying to somehow pin it down with my presence so it wouldn't disappear entirely. Eventually I took up a weekly volunteer shift at a local food bank where I was wrapped up in so much protective gear, I looked like one of those fearsome scientists from *E.T.* who come to inspect him.

And so, the second Ellie tells her Fruitz story, my ears prick up like a dog who has heard the word *bone*. I want to know more.

She says it's like Tinder. But less serious if that's possible. I make a sandwich of the gooey *chèvre* between two pieces of salami and ask her to explain it.

Fruitz is divided into four fruit categories.

Cherry is "to find your other half." Grape "for a glass of wine with no trouble." Watermelon is "no seeds attached." Peach is "to meet people who are looking for the same kind of relationship you are."

"That's straight hookup," says Ellie. "It's all straight hookup, but the messages are dirtier if you're a peach."

I have already begun downloading the app.

"What fruit should I pick?" I ask the group, turning the phone screen around and showing the table.

"I can't believe it's called Fruitz," says Nina. "It's so ridiculous."

Nina can so easily pass for American that sometimes the only way to remember she's Finnish is from encounters with her practical side, which runs as deep and cold as Finnish winter nights. Nina tells the story of the time, shortly before lockdown began, when she briefly dated a man who liked to take her out for $400 meals. "Where the *Obamas* dined!" she'll say disbelievingly. She hated it: "He barely knows me, why is he spending so much money on me."

I'm happy to concede to Nina that this dating app *is* ridiculous. Indeed, most of the time I'm grateful for her levelheadedness. But nothing about my presence here is practical. And all dating apps are ridiculous, by and large, there's no arguing with that. But I shrug off the concern. One of the unexpected realizations to come out of my forties is that being human is often largely ridiculous. This, and that how we experience romance at age fifteen is more or less the same as romance at eighty-five. The assumption that we ever move on from giddy insecurity in the face of attraction to some more stoic and balanced response seems to me either an illusion created from a vacuum of storytelling, or the triumph of cynicism. Actual maturity, I've come to suspect, is largely just succeeding at not letting the injuries of your childhood debilitate you, which is the great challenge of life. As Larkin says, "An only life can take so long to climb / clear of its wrong beginnings, and may never." We're all mostly just sending the same messages back and forth to each other from puberty to death, the only difference as we go (hopefully) being that we do so with a better understanding of what we want, what we need, and the ability to ask for it directly and walk away from it more quickly when it doesn't serve us.

There have been times when I can't differentiate between the exchanges my newly divorced (and sometimes not yet divorced, though clearly heading in that direction) friends show me they are having with prospective partners/hookups and the texts teenagers (sometimes their own teenagers) in my life show me they are exchanging with their crushes. If anything, the former could learn from the latter. Which is to say, of the truly ridiculous things that have been revealed about human behavior in the last two years, hurling myself onto a ludicrously premised dating app hardly ranks. It's a means to an end.

I don't really have any photos, though, is the issue. I have outfits galore, but no photos. The ones on my long-neglected Tinder account are now two years old. I scroll through my most recent album hoping to scrape something up that shows me in an appealing light. Most of the photos I have of myself are selfies of me inspecting my face in the light of the window. Here's a series where I'm marking my various stages of gray. I've had a small patch of gray in the middle of my scalp since I was a teenager; the result, I was once told by a hairdresser, of damaged follicles probably from being hit by a fly ball at a Blue Jays baseball game when I was younger. I've been coloring that spot regularly for as long as I can remember. During the lockdown, when I ceased to maintain just about everything, I discovered that the "spot" had expanded, like weeds, and gray was now sprouting up everywhere.

Here, too, are the close shots of my forehead—were fine lines finally emerging? And my neck—no matter what angle or light I catch it in, it's clear twenty years of careful care had not warded off Nora Ephron's truths.

I keep scrolling. A series of Zoom screenshots. My face shrinks to a box in the lower corner of the screen. Here is me laughing with various children—my nieces and nephews, my army of godchildren—who are demonstrating to me their coloring, their new dance moves, new outfits, new maps, new trucks *the size of a Megalodon*, the dinner they are eating, the book they are reading, the game they are extremely good at. My face morphs into exaggerated eyes and a round mouth as I attempt to interact with the babies peering into the screen as though they might climb through. There are a few group photos, multiple squares all over the screen, like a distorted opening of *The Brady Bunch*, from the regular Thursday calls with the people I waited tables with in the Village twenty years ago. Here are the shots of the Paris calls. Of my writing group. As I was trying to convince myself

I still exist in the realm of other people. In all of these I am in my pajamas. A sweatshirt. A bathrobe. Leaned into the corner of the couch, the side table lamp harsh on one side of my face, casting the other in shadow. At my small kitchen table, my hair an unwashed halo about my head, the sink and the cupboards directly behind me, my fridge plastered with printed versions of the people these screengrabs contain.

None of this is going on a dating app for which I have just registered myself as a watermelon.

Finally, I stumble on some mirror selfies snapped ten days ago. During New York's brief frenzied reentry into normalcy, and after a gauntlet of vaccine checks and mask requirements, I'd gone to a premiere for a television show a friend was involved in. It was in an old theater in Midtown, three quarters of the seats intentionally left empty. The downstairs ladies' room had an old-fashioned lounge, a large room with tall, narrow mirrors lining one wall, framed with light bulbs as though everyone in it was backstage preparing for the curtain to rise. It was empty. I'd donned my mask-proof red Maybelline lipstick, visible in the photo because, alone in the room, I'd pulled my mask off, though I'm intentionally holding it in my hand so that it's visible in all the shots. Even alone, I felt compelled to demonstrate I was still thinking of the well-being of others. That I believed in science. Behind me, golden light. Leather chairs. Carpeting. Red lips. My hair.

One of these photos will have to do for now. I select one and find another I took in the elevator mirror in my building—a full-length one that shows off my entire body, even though my face is covered in a mask. If you want to enter a meat market, be prepared to show the meat.

I show these to the table.

"Is that really all you have?"

"Your hair looks great, anyway."

"Are you sure you want to put your real age?"

The truth is, I could probably list myself as ten years younger and get away with it. And not just because of hair dye, as Nora E. claimed (though it does contribute). But why? I'm not ten years younger. During lockdown, I could have written ten essays about the theft that has been committed on my time and mind by the belief I need to look better, younger, thinner. There were weeks last winter when, desperate for a sense of comradeship, for the feel of a crowd, to remind myself what anticipation felt like, I pulled out all the photos I had that showed me at parties with friends. I looked amazing in all of them. I couldn't believe it. I dazzled. And yet, I'm aware that in each instance I'd been horrified by the photos the first time I'd seen them. The disconnect is staggering to me now. When I mention this to a friend, she says it's just that we are attracted to youth. But I don't think that's totally it. Certainly, I'm now able to enjoy the very obviously unflattering photos from two decades ago the way we all feel compassion and humor about something painful that is now so out of reach. It's the other photos I'm reacting to, the ones that, by any measure, show me to be the woman I knew I had been trying so hard to be but never understood until now that I had been all along. For weeks I stared at these photos the way my mother used to devour celebrity magazines, as if I might still be able to possess some of that vitality and beauty if I just spent enough time consuming it. Eventually, I did some calculations and concluded that there is, on average, a five-year gap between current me being able to enjoy the me in the photos. Five years before I can clearly see myself for what I am: powerful and alive and beautiful. Ever since, when I see a photo of myself, as much as I may be put off by it (and there is plenty to be put off by, as this recent tour through my phone has evidenced) I remind myself that in five years I will love it. But I don't want to wait five years. I want enjoyment now. Lying about my age on this absurd app strikes me as voluntarily enacting a theft upon myself. I'm a forty-six-year-old writer in Paris for a month. My hard work and mind and experience have brought me here against not a few odds. I'm not going to wait five years to enjoy it. I'm not going to relinquish any of those years to make someone feel better about enjoying me.

Am I sure I want to put my real age?

"Fuck yeah, I am."

I walk home through empty, silent Paris. It is equal parts familiar and strange. My feet know the way, but my mind is still having a hard time grasping that I'm actually here.

My earlier, misguided nap takes its revenge on me and once in bed I'm unable to sleep. I reach for the phone and decide this is as good a time as any to update all the dating apps, which now number three: Bumble, Tinder, and now Fruitz.

I go through each and update them to the same parameters:

Bio: New Yorker, 46, à Paris pour un mois.

Age range I am open to: 28–58.

Distance: 5 miles (8 kilometers). In New York this is tricky because on the Upper West Side I'm five miles away from parts of Jersey that culturally could be two or three time zones away. But Paris is a circle and small. And I'm close enough to the center of it.

Gender: Male. I've been with women, and from time to time I've opened this up to women, but it's not what I'm looking for right now.

As I'm doing this, my phone buzzes. It takes me a minute to figure out why. Ah, someone has messaged me on Fruitz. That was fast.

The first thing that catches my eye is the word *masseur.* I'm unsure what the rest says—I only see the words *masseur* and *très gentil.* They translate into my head as gentle stroking, which is correct in the spirit of things, if not the letter of translation. I look at the photos—there is a feather, a velvet glove—which back up my conclusion that whatever is being offered will involve a lot of touching.

Masseur is older, than me anyway, fifty-two, with close-cropped hair and a receding hairline. The photos show only half his face. He's wearing a mask. But what I *can* see is handsome, in the older, confident way. I read the bio again. He is *"très sympathique,"* which I know does not translate directly into sympathetic, but nonetheless leaves me with that impression. I spot the word *indulgente.* Leave it to the French to find the right language. A sympathetic person who wants to indulge me with a lot of touch. Seek and ye shall find, I think, smiling.

It's past midnight, and I'm alone in bed on my first night in Paris with rosé coursing through my veins. I swipe right and send one of the basic prompt questions the app provides: Does he prefer *vin ou bière?* It is the most innocuous question I can find.

My phone vibrates again almost immediately. The Masseur prefers wine. A longer message immediately follows:

"*Bonjour* Glynnis, do you prefer English?"

"*Oui*," I type back.

"I love New York," he says. "What are you doing in Paris for a month? Vacationing?"

"Seeing friends and working," I type back. My desire to be anything but a tourist on holiday overrides my instinct to not share too much information with strangers on a French dating app where everyone has consented to be a fruit.

"How wonderful. Your first time?"

It absolutely is not, I think. But I write: "*Non*, I come here every summer, but last, of course."

"How nice."

I think so too. But before I can respond, another message comes through.

"And what are you looking for here, Glynnis?"

God bless the French for their directness.

And yet, the question feels weighted in ways I am unprepared for. It momentarily drags me out of my body.

How long had it been since someone had asked me about my wants and needs? This trip had been largely motivated by the desire for movement. The sensation of hurling myself into the world and being seen. To feel alive. And now I was being asked to see myself in a very different way.

What *am* I looking for here?

I close my eyes. I think of all the photos I spent time looking at this last year of people together, the deep loneliness of being able to see, but not touch. I think of massages. I think of shared meals. I think of not being the scaffolding on other people's lives, at least for a few weeks. Of being *selfish*, that most damning of words. I think of receiving instead of giving.

What am I here for?

"I'm mostly here to enjoy myself," I type back.

FIVE

Pass Sanitaire

Befor any real enjoyment can occur, I need a *pass sanitaire*. The French are about to implement strict vaccination rules in the hopes of getting their numbers down. No one will be allowed anywhere but to grocery shop without the pass—no cafés, no *boulangeries*. This is the threat, anyway. There has been some skepticism about whether this will actually be enforced, but the general sense is it will, at least in the short term. There is a strong anti-vax movement in France, and Macron is determined to stamp it out. He's made it clear he's willing to go to extremes to do so. American paper vaccination cards may be accepted? May not? There's no official word.

When Nina tells me this on our WhatsApp group chat before I leave New York, I don't give it much thought. The borders are open. "Presumably, they will have to have guidelines for the tourists," I write back.

"LOL," comes the reply.

Each week the deadline gets pushed one more week. But the official word now is this will all go into effect next Monday, six days from now. *Certainement* this time. Rumors fly around Facebook about how it might be implemented for non-EU citizens, but still nothing official. Somehow even in this overly connected world, Paris feels like a lunchroom game of telephone, rumors rolling around until they gain enough momentum to be facts. Like a city about to be under occupation, those who want out have left or are leaving; those who are staying are trying to establish their means of movement.

"I told you," says Nina. "You've forgotten French bureaucracy. They have no guidelines. They don't care about what's practical."

Through this cloud of hazy information floats the promise of one *pharmacie* at Opéra that is transferring the American vaccination cards to the digital *pass sanitaire*. Is there anything more American than a paper vaccination card in a digital age? Bureaucracy as isolationism.

An American friend of Nina's had apparently been to this pharmacy only the week before and secured the *pass*. Aarti's office is across the street and she's seen the line. Everyone seems to know someone who's gone there. What I need is a French address, which I have. Once I provide this, they will put my info into the system, register me, give me a printout with a QR code that I will scan into an app, and voilà (here, literally, *voilà*), I will have the *pass sanitaire*.

I need to prove permanence to move freely.

It's now my second day in Paris. I wake up starving. But I'm craving dinner, not breakfast. My stomach is still somewhere over the Atlantic.

The smell of garlic once again floating through the window does not help the confusion. On the way home from drinks the night before, I'd stopped at the Carrefour and picked up the basics: coffee, yogurt, muesli. My usual staples now in French packaging. So at least breakfast is easily accessible.

The church bells go off. I count the rings instead of looking at my phone. It's 10:00 a.m. I have slept through the earlier rounds: they start at 8:00 a.m., ringing every hour until 10:00 p.m., or 22h00. When I'm on deadline it's a useful way to keep me focused. The original Pomodoro method. I'd intended to get an early start in case there was a line up at the Opéra *pharmacie*, perhaps meet Aarti, who is back in the office, for a croissant beforehand. But there's no point in rushing now. I make my coffee and eat my yogurt and muesli. The bells are on their eleventh ring as I walk out the door.

I head toward Bastille, noting again the absence of people on Rue de la Roquette. Normally it's loud and boisterous. Now the sidewalks are almost completely empty. It's like the last year was a sort of tsunami that swept so much away, starting with the most vulnerable.

I cross the enormous roundabout without having to wait for a light change; once Saint-Antoine shifts into Rivoli I stop at a *boulangerie* and get a quiche. The sense that I have only just been here and only just done this is overwhelming.

I eat while I walk. People will tell you the French never eat and walk. But it's not true. The culture of rush is less prevalent here, but it's here.

The heaviness of the pastry. All the different ways the butter and cream have been conspired into this solid disc, are exactly what my stomach needs to settle me into this timeline. They reach out and drag my body from where it is still hovering hours behind me, and plunk it down here, on Rue de Rivoli at 11h45 Paris time.

I look for a Vélib', Paris's public bike-share program. The app has remained on my phone since my last trip in December 2019 when I'd traveled here on a $300 plane ticket, bought on a whim during a seat sale. Despite not being able to go anywhere, or maybe because of it, I'd continued to renew my membership since then. Even when I'm not here, I sometimes open the Vélib' app and observe the number of bikes rise and fall at the stations I use most often, a sense of the city inhaling and exhaling even when I'm not there to breathe with it.

The bike lanes have been widened since last I rode them. Now half of Rue du Rivoli, the main east-west thoroughfare on the Right Bank, is devoted to *les bicyclettes*. Not long ago bikes in Paris felt like an afterthought, but each year there are more helmets on the road, a sign that biking has been absorbed into daily life as a thing to be taken seriously. Once, many years ago, I stood on the west side of Place de la Concorde staring ahead across the many lanes of traffic, with cars zooming into and around it at top speed. In the distance was the Tuileries and beyond that the shadowy outline of the Louvre. Through this opera of automobiles, a woman on a bike with a basket full of groceries sailed past. She was erect, slim, probably in her forties, her hair in a bun and no helmet or sunglasses. Calmly pedaling her way back home with enormous composure and confidence. She stands out in my memory because when I laid eyes on her, smoothly navigating her way through the careening metal vehicles, I immediately thought, That is what I want to be, whatever *that* is. I couldn't have articulated it at the time, but when I think of it now, the word *singular* comes to mind. She somehow evoked a future I wanted to be heading toward.

I stop at the first Vélib' stand and find a bike whose seat is raised higher than normal, a sign that it has been used recently and should, theoretically, be working. I type in my code. It works. A surge of triumph. A bike pass, in any city, seems like a measure of a life well lived.

Having prosaic things to do in an operatic city is one definition of what it is to be European. The *pharmacie* I have been directed toward, as if it were the last functioning gas station in a city under siege, is located across from the Opéra Métro. There are only a few cars out. The sidewalks are sparse.

I lock the bike at another stand and walk the stretch of storefronts three times, looking for the line I assume I will encounter since the location is being passed around expat Facebook accounts right now. Life has been a series of lines for more than a year. Lines into the grocery. Lines outside the H&H hospital on the Upper East Side to get tested. Lines into the American Museum of Natural History to be vaccinated. But I see no one. Finally, seeing no other option I go back to the small *pharmacie* at the address I've been given but have assumed is incorrect because when I pass it the first time it is empty. Google Maps is never entirely reliable in France. For reasons I suspect have to do with strict privacy laws, the country has not fully attached itself to the internet like some sort of capitalist leech. Hours and locations here are more suggestions than anything else. Especially in August.

The *pharmacie* is open. Something that's never a guarantee in

August either. The short aisles are empty, but there's a tall young man with dark hair, and a young woman behind the counter. Neither is wearing the white lab coats you often see in a French *pharmacie*, which gives me pause. The woman greets me in French. I don't even bother to pretend that I can get through what I need in French and promptly tell her, in English, that I am looking to transfer my American vaccination card to the *pass sanitaire*. She smiles and shakes her head and glances at her co-worker. The young man steps forward from the shelves he is restocking and says, "Yes?" The question mark is barely pronounced.

I repeat myself.

He also shakes his head. They no longer do it, he says. I must go to the American embassy. The American embassy? I wonder if I am hearing correctly. This is new. Yes, he says, all the *pharmacies* got a call yesterday to stop transferring the American cards and send everyone there. I try to imagine someone calling all the pharmacies in Paris to pass on this information—it may have been a translation blip, but it's not unimaginable. This is France, bureaucracy is practically a religion; it's not all that hard to believe there is a person in a room somewhere with a long list dialing away on an actual phone. At the same time, I recognize the tone of a person who has been dealing with long lineups for days. I recognize the Frenchness of this conversation. I almost never encounter the rudeness Parisians have been made famous for by culture—maybe it's generational, maybe it's the fact I am almost always on my own—but I can tell I'm on the edge of it here. I sense myself at the end of a long line of Americans having this exact conversation, in larger groups and different tones. I feel the reverberations of them ramming up against the French love of rules.

I feel myself getting tipped into the bottomless pit of French red tape I have managed to avoid in almost all forms until now. I understand there is no more help to be had here. It is not possible to charm one's way out of the French social net.

I thank them and leave.

"Why would you have to go to the American embassy?" messages Nina. "It's a French pass, the Americans won't be allowed to give it out."

"No idea," I type back, though I hadn't thought of this. "But there's nothing to be done here." I repeat what he told me about the call going out. "I'm going to walk over and see."

"Ridiculous," comes the response. Nina, also a lover of rules, has no tolerance for absurd ones.

Perhaps one way to measure a life is by how many trips to an embassy one has been required to make. I live in the United States, a country I am not yet a citizen of, and yet I have made none. Even when I acquired my green card it merely involved one visit to what had, at that point, somewhat recently been renamed Homeland Security, the Orwellian nature of the moniker underscored by the large portraits of George W. Bush and Dick Cheney smiling—or more accurately, in the latter's case, grimacing—down upon everyone who entered. The building was in the part of Long Island that maintained the nondescript bleakness of the outer reaches of the boroughs, and once inside everyone else who was there for processing made the assumption, based on my skin color and lack of accent, that I was an employee and began asking me questions. My official meeting lasted all of three minutes.

The American embassy in Paris is just off the Champs-Élysées gardens, across from the western corner of the Place de la Concorde. It is not nondescript. Indeed, it's difficult to imagine a *more* descript place. To the left, a glimpse of the Arc de Triomphe, to the right, the Louvre. Across the street is the Crillon. It is a love letter to Parisian real estate. It is easier to understand the Second World War as recent history when you encounter the prime placement of American figures—and often the renaming of boulevards and squares after FDR or JFK—in European capitals. And then ponder if, once that history becomes less recent, or the Americans too intolerable, they will be returned to their original names, like St. Petersburg or Volgograd, and the embassy converted to some sort of museum as an act of redemption or retribution.

Right now it seems an unlikely place for such a minor transaction as the *pass sanitaire* conversion, but faith in the obscurity of French bureaucracy propels me on. Also, I see a long line snaking down Avenue Gabriel. Ah yes, this seems more like it. I spot a young guard watching me. He gives me a charming grin and a wave. How I have missed flirting. The simple act of charming your way through an interaction. Of having potential in the eyes of another. I try my luck. "*Pass sanitaire?*" I call. He frowns sympathetically. I call it again. He shrugs and points me toward the line. I'm tempted to stay here and see whether this brief interaction might lead to something more— would he be a watermelon, or a cherry?—but the line looks long. And I get the sense the clock is ticking.

I navigate a fortress of barricades to no avail. A quick confused conversation with the guards managing the tent in front of the embassy, under the beseeching eyes of that long line, and it's quickly clear no one here has any idea what I'm talking about. What is clear is that everyone in line is (a) French and (b) waiting hopefully for a visa to the US. This all makes sense, of course. This is the American embassy. I am the thing that doesn't make sense.

"Of course they can't give it to you," messages Nina. "It's a ridiculous thing to tell people."

Her indignation has the effect of making me feel less foolish. At least I didn't stand in that line all day.

Another location has popped up on the Facebook groups that Nina is monitoring for me from her apartment in the 11th as she files her stories for the day. She has a regular gig covering television for a Canadian publication that is somehow still in business. She takes a screengrab of the Facebook post and sends it to me. According to the latest word-of-mouth update, they are doing conversions at the Hôtel Dieu Hospital. I google map it and see its location across the street from Notre-Dame. Can that be right? "Yep," says Nina.

It's 12:30 p.m. I'm tempted to go home and sleep—I'm already tired out from the riding and walking, and more drinks with everyone have been scheduled for 18h00. Still, I can't shake the sense that I'm on some sort of treasure hunt. That it's very likely the thing I am searching for will cease to exist tomorrow. The experience of having things disappear overnight has become normalized enough that I know it's entirely possible I may wake up tomorrow to a city that is barricaded against me. That every plan I've made, from friends to cheese to nudity, hinges on my figuring this out *immédiatement*. It's this that propels me on.

I'm halfway to the Louvre when I look up and force myself to stop and take it all in. I am in the Tuileries! Not alone, but surely with fewer people than have been here in, how long? Before, empty cities seemed to be a phenomenon created by apocalypse movies, or weather. The long rows of flowers, exploding into bloom. The faint floral scent. The sense I am in a painting. I keep walking, trying not to let my mind wander.

I know my way to Notre-Dame without mapping. Through the arch. Along the Seine. Over to the island. The cathedral is still under scaffolding from the fire that toppled the steeple. It looks like it's under a shroud.

During my first lonely month in Paris, in the summer of 2016 shortly after I'd sold my first book, I would leave the apartment at night, the same one I'm in now, and walk the narrow streets. Deep in the terror of a first draft, I would come upon the cathedral from the side, the tourist shops shuttered for the evening, and then stand in the square and try to get a perfectly symmetrical photo of the façade, using my proximity to the monument as evidence to myself that I was capable of finishing a book I wasn't entirely sure I understood how to write.

My current sense of capability diminishes as I circle Notre-Dame. The barricades around the cathedral complicate matters, as does what appears to be a tent, though no one is in it. My phone tells me I'm standing in front of the Hôtel Dieu, but none of the doors seem to lead anywhere useful. Is this an actual hospital? Or was it once a hospital and is now something else, like the Hôtel des Invalides, where I once saw an opera? History has perverted the meaning of language here. These are short streets surrounding the cathedral; I don't even know if they have names. This is the old pre-Haussmann Paris, one that survived the bulldozing, envisioned and executed to eradicate the health issues that plagued the poor neighborhoods. Now the streets are lined with little shops selling racks of trinkets. It's the trinkets right now that feel like an advertisement of the past more than the buildings.

Across from the hospital is a large stone arch that in past years I've seen people lined up at, overseen by severe-looking guards. I think it might be a courthouse. There is no one there now, but maybe that is where I am supposed to be? If I continue on this way I will just end up back on Rivoli not far from where I had my first quiche, and if I go in the opposite direction, I will cross the bridge to the Left Bank and be in sight of Shakespeare and Company. I am technically in tourist central. Having a government office here is like if the American consulate were located in Times Square. Which I suppose is a possibility; Paris is either less segregated when it comes to tourists than New York, or more overrun everywhere, depending how you look at it.

I navigate my way along the tents, thinking I may spot someone official looking. And it's here that I come upon modern glass sliding doors that I've never noticed before, but which have the prescriptive appearance of a place connected to health.

The security guard nods when I pass, and the woman behind the desk points me in the direction of a door. "To get my *pass sanitaire*," I say in English. "Yes," she tells me. I clock the absence of any confusion on her face and it gives me a thrill. "Through that door and to your right," she says, pointing. It seems too simple. I walk through the lobby as directed, and through the next door. There is a little white room on the right with four people inside, a young man and a woman and an older couple holding papers. The young man looks up at me. "Can I convert my American vaccination to a *pass sanitaire*?" I ask, again in English. He nods, *pleasantly*, yes. Wonderful! "Wait outside and we will call you in," he says. I step back into the doorway frame. "No," he says, and points back to the lobby, *à gauche*. I walk back and look to the left. Along the window ledge, there is a line of people sitting. All eyes are casually resting on me, the way pets will sit by a window and keep an eye on what passes by. I smile. "Is this the line?" I ask in English. Nods. I've never been so happy to see a line. There is just enough space for me to sit down at the end next to an older woman who is by herself.

Older woman. In my own head I am still young. I do not yet feel the diminishment of my so-called powers in the way I have been warned will happen. Far from invisible, I do not feel even remotely faded. I wonder sometimes if this is because I live by myself and do not have the experience of living alongside people whom I have loved enough to commit my life to, have birthed, have raised through the years of total dependence, who have defined my place in the world, and who suddenly, or slowly and then quickly, need me less. See me less. I have only myself to see me. I once wrote a short story in my twenties about a girl (me, obviously) whose only understanding of herself was her reflection in the windows of stores she walked past. My writing teacher was not as impressed as I wanted her to be. But I often think back to that observation. I am often defined to myself by my impression of my own reflection. Never more so than in the past fourteen months. Do the people next to me now consider me an older woman? Did the young, impatient man at the *pharmacie?* Am I mistaking the disinterest that I'm warned comes with age for Frenchness? Most of my interactions with young women since turning forty leave me with the impression that I am their coveted research subject, and they are taking notes; far from discarded, they seem to be holding on to me tightly. But we've all been out of circulation for a while now. Perhaps I've reemerged into the world *middle-aged*, not just numbers-wise but spiritually, publicly. Maybe I'm in my era of invisibility and just don't know it. It is admittedly difficult to feel a loss of power when one is sitting two hundred feet from Notre-Dame Cathedral having hurled oneself across an ocean with no guarantee of a smooth return. But I consider the possibility.

I have time to contemplate all this as I watch people arrive and retrace my steps: in the door, to the desk, questions repeated, almost always in English, fingers pointed, across the lobby, into the small room, and eventually back out again to the waiting line of casually resting eyes. Each time someone new takes on the task of affirming that, yes, this is the line. There is a brief moment between the new addition disappearing into the hallway and reappearing, when everyone tenses up. Has this interloper been served while we all wait out here? No one stops them on their way in though, including me; we only direct them to the end of the line when they reemerge.

I message Nina and Sandra. "Hôtel Dieu FTW. In line!" This will get passed on and added to the word-of-mouth chain on Facebook.

Nina responds with three emoji thumbs-ups. Sandra says, *"Bonne chance."*

I try to gauge how quickly the line is moving. Each person is inside for an average of fifteen minutes. At this rate I will be here for three hours, which seems like not the worst bargain, though my phone battery is already half dead and idiotically I have not brought a book. Near the front of the line there is a family of Americans, blonde and white and exactly what the world believes Americans to be. Paris may feel empty, but I am hardly the only American to make this trip. Not surprising, I suppose, when at least half the country decided Covid was over a year ago.

I learned long ago to say New York City when people ask me where I'm from; it's proven the fastest route to garnering whatever shred of respect a traveler might expect—more even than whatever goodwill I can expect from my Canadian passport—and the only place the Parisians will concede is on their level. New York exists as an idea to almost everyone, everywhere. An appealing idea. An exciting one. Including to me sometimes, despite having nearly twenty-five years of actual lived time there. Whether or not that idea has any truth to it, enough people believe it that it becomes its own powerful, universally understood language. And my mother tongue.

I only last ten minutes before striking up a conversation with the older woman next to me. I have become a person who strikes up conversations. With the people at the checkout in Fairway. With the women who work at the post office. More than at any other time, I remind myself of my mother when I do this. So much of my childhood was spent in a state of indignation and mortification over my mother chatting with strangers. Making pleasantries with the checkout person. The teacher. Slowing down our return to the family room television set. It's only in the past few months, as I find myself holding

64

conversations about weather, and shopping, and my niece and nephews to whom this package is addressed, that I understand all this small talk as a symptom of loneliness and am able to recognize the shape of my mother's isolation.

I discover the older woman beside me is from Eastern Europe and is trying to convert her husband's vaccination card into a *pass sanitaire*. Her husband is from Morocco, and he is supposed to arrive tomorrow. He needs this conversion in order to stay, is what I am able to glean between the fractured English and our masks. She's concerned she won't be able to do this for him.

I can feel her desperation and anxiety. I can't tell whether the anxiety is about him or the people in the office. I feel like I've spent the entire year witnessing women acting on behalf of the men in their lives, being stretched further and further, pulled beyond their limits. Is that what's happening here? Or is this paperwork anxiety? I have no way of knowing.

She is an anomaly in this group, which is otherwise clearly made up of tourists.

The line snakes along.

To my left is another white American couple. I can tell they're from the northern Midwest simply by their reticence. They are friendly, but not quick to conversation. Talking to Americans is a tricky business these days; the safe ground of casual conversation has become increasingly narrow and requires some sniffing around as though two alpha dogs are meeting and deciding on whether to fight. The shared experience of citizenship that might have once buoyed one through a casual conversation is gone and been replaced by knives. At home the absence of a mask is usually a clear sign of one's affiliations, like some sort of gang patch or tattoo, but here everyone must wear one still. It would probably be easier to stay silent, but I'm too curious to know how they found their way here; were they also told that the American embassy was doing these conversions? Yes, they were. They also got this address from Facebook. They are here for a week. The conversation dies. I watch more people come in and repeat the steps. There is no more room on the ledge.

The older woman to my right continues to shuffle through her papers with an increasingly nervous energy I recognize from time spent in immigration rooms, time spent standing in line to get my green card renewed. I see the familiar demeanor of a person needing to be recognized in order to literally exist in this space.

It worries me I have not brought my green card with me on this odyssey. It's back at the flat. It rarely leaves the house unless absolutely necessary. By law I am supposed to carry it everywhere in America; I never do. Better to risk the fine that comes with not having it on me than go through the expensive, monthslong rigmarole of replacing it. This is a rule I implemented for myself after I was once mugged—less a mugging than a purse snatching to be more accurate—by a kid on a bike in broad daylight on the Eastern Parkway promenade in Brooklyn. It all happened so quickly that I stood stunned as I watched him ride off with my bag (and my green card).

When I filed a police report later that afternoon, the officers kept asking me about valuables, how much money was on me. Did they take my computer? I didn't care. I only wanted them to know I was now without my green card. Its absence had returned me to a person with questionable status, faded me out of the picture. "You're lucky," the officer said (here my memory can't commit to one version—he either said I was lucky or that I was smart). "A lot of folks up in Harlem and the Bronx get violently injured putting up a fight for theirs when they're robbed." He said it like they were foolish not to just let it go, in the way one talks about cash or jewelry. Possessions not being as important as your life. But what is the life of a nonperson in the eyes of the law? What is one willing to risk for the right to move freely? Or to remain safely in a place? Not that I was overly fearful of either of these things. There was, on any given day, a less than zero chance anyone in New York was going to ask me, a white woman with American-sounding English, to prove I had the right to be in New York.

When I returned to Homeland Security a few months later to be refingerprinted for my replacement card, one of the officials taking my papers briefly got aggressive with me. "What happened to your green card?" he asked in an accusing tone, hovering over me where I sat, as if I had casually thrown it in the garbage. Without giving it a thought, I snapped back. "I got mugged!" Then I turned my back on him. He came around and apologized and asked me if I was okay. It was then I realized, no amount of paper can replace the deep confidence that comes from a lifetime of being given the benefit of the doubt.

I wonder if I should leave to retrieve my green card from the flat. But that seems foolish. This place may be shut by the time I return. The line closed. This may not even exist as an option tomorrow. I will take my chances, I decide. I have a Canadian passport and a New York City vaccination card that, even though it looks as though it might have been issued sometime in the late seventies, is still official. I'm hard-pressed to think of a single place in which one or the other doesn't work in one's favor.

The loud blonde American family up front finally goes in. We all watch them and I can feel the group's mental calculation over whether their togetherness will slow the line or speed it up. This fresh anxiety is mitigated by the fact we all get to move down the ledge by a few feet. Even this brief sensation of movement is encouraging. More people sit down. The American father emerges only a few minutes later and turns to the line. "They want to know the date you got your last shot and which arm," he tells us without being asked. One never fully realizes how friendly Americans are until one is outside the country. The woman beside me starts texting furiously into her phone. Then she picks it up and begins talking furiously in French. It's a short conversation, and when she hangs up she shrugs and mumbles to herself.

Shortly the rest of the family appears. That was fast. A ripple of energy. We all move up. This is going quickly now. The woman beside me is ushered in, not more than five minutes has passed since the Americans have left. "Good luck," I say. She nods and scurries in. But she comes out just as quickly. The look on her face tells me everything. "He must be here," she says to my inquiring glance, and shrugs. It's the shrug of a person accustomed to obstacles and paperwork. "*Bonne chance.*" She waves and is out the door.

In I go.

I already have my passport and vaccination card out, sensitive to the waiting eyes outside along the window ledge.

"I'm Canadian," I say immediately.

I elaborate quickly: "But I was vaccinated in New York City, because I live there. I have my New York driver's license if that helps." I figure it's better for everyone if I just lay it all out.

I brace.

A few summers ago, Aarti and Nina were trying to plan a holiday and struggling to find an island they wanted to go to, one Aarti could also travel to without needing to apply for a visa. "You need a visa to travel there?" I recall asking with the obliviousness that can come from never having to consider whether I'm free to go somewhere. Of never having my citizenship be thought of in any way but as a story the world was happy to hear, whether or not that legitimacy was earned.

"I need a visa to go anywhere," Aarti said evenly. And then pointedly: "*Most* people do."

The young man who had redirected me to the lobby when I first arrived, shrugs. "That's fine," he says in English.

I hand him the cards, preparing for more questions.

"I want to go to New York so badly," he says. "My cousin lives there."

Now this is a language I am fluent in.

His cousin lives upstate it turns out. He tries to explain to me where, and I nod along though I have no idea of the town he's referring to. I encourage him to go. "It's beautiful there," I say.

"I once went to Brooklyn," he tells me, typing in the information on my vaccination card. "I will save up to go again. Plane tickets are expensive."

"So expensive," I say. "It's crazy." It's true, my flight in the cheapest seat I could find had cost me twelve hundred dollars. Nearly twice what I was accustomed to paying.

He hands me a piece of paper and points to a QR code. "You can download the app and scan this code for your phone. That will be your pass."

I'm stunned. I've been here maybe four minutes.

"That's all?"

"*Oui, c'est fini.*" He's already turning back to his desk.

"*Très bien. Merci beaucoup. Bonne journée.*" I string together what little French I currently have, and all my New York energy gets injected into it.

"*Bonne journée,*" he says with a big smile.

I emerge buoyed by the immediate satisfaction of being recognized by the state. I'm official.

I smile at the line, but I have no information to share, I was not asked for anything, not even which arm. All I can offer is speediness. The line shuffles again as I exit and reemerge onto the square. I was inside for fifty-five minutes.

"*Fini!*" I message the group and make my way back along the quiet side street, the tall walls of Notre-Dame in silent mourning beside me.

Paris is now my oyster. And how does one consume an oyster? You slurp it up.

No Seeds Attached

My god, there are so many messages waiting for me. In the course of the few days I've been here my phone has turned into a mobile *Penthouse Letters*. Immediately when I open Fruitz, a series of "crush notes" pop up. This, I learn, means someone has paid extra to skip the line, as it were, and contact me directly. Today the first one says "beautiful eyes" in English. The sender is thirty years old. I heart him. Hearting someone on Fruitz is the same as swiping right . . . I think. It's consenting to open up the relationship (so-called) to direct conversation. Another crush note, this one also in English: "if you want pleasure with a good boy, im here." Twenty-six years old. A bit much. Another one, this one from an interesting-looking forty-eight-year-old, asking me if I want to go away for the weekend. "Hello Glynnis . . . *Je cherche une partenaire de voyage pour 4 jours fin août sur Carcassonne?* Are you ready? *Musique et gastronomie sont au . . .*"

I am most definitely not in New York anymore. Part of translating French, or any language, presumably, is obviously not just translating the words. It is grasping the underlying meaning, the spirit versus the letter. When it comes to French, French men mean what they say. At least at first. And they tend to say it immediately, and persistently. This is often an utterly foreign concept for a New Yorker when it comes to dating, where oftentimes the assumption is that men don't mean a single thing they say. And never say what they mean. French men, in my experience, anyway, are all in almost immediately. There is an absence of sarcasm and irony, which can telegraph as sincerity. It's this male French persistence that often gets American women in trouble. They mistake the immediacy for longevity. Think they've found the love the movies have promised them, only to find out after a few years their great love has discovered another great love and now they are entangled in the French legal system of divorce and custody, which is another sort of permanence, entirely, and one far less invested in the enjoyment of women. I have encountered more than a few American women now permanently tethered to France in ways they did not anticipate and are very much not enjoying.

I'm not here for permanence though. I look up Carcassonne in Google Maps. It's a picturesque resort town to the south in the mountains. I swipe right. Perhaps I *am* interested in going to Carcassonne for four days. All the attention feels like pure oxygen. Anything is possible.

I'm catching up on these messages in Parc Monceau. I've been in Paris four or five days now. The jet lag has receded. The shock of being in another place has settled into familiarity. Around me Parisians are sprinkled across the grass in little pockets of color. The trees overhead are a gently swaying canopy of green. Above, blue sky. Squint the eyes a bit and I suppose I could be in a Seurat painting. Or a scene from a Henry James novel. But I'm not a portrait either man would likely recognize. I'm a forty-six-year-old woman—not married, no children—currently perusing a French dating app called Fruitz.

I'm not prepared to be this desired. Even though I have asked for it, so to speak, I did not expect so many to answer. Who or what are they all responding to? I scroll back through my own profile and try to get a sense of what others are seeing. I've been staring at my own face on a screen for so long it's difficult to see it at all. I've lost any sense of what it telegraphs, I can only translate it to myself with the language I've been given to use. The fine lines. The softening upper arms. The head tilted at an angle that suggests a jawline that perhaps does not exactly materialize in life. I have no idea. My image has become a word that, said too many times in a row, loses all meaning. I go back through the most appealing messages and type *merci* to the ones written in English and thank you to ones written in French. *"Bien,"* I say to the man voyaging to Carcassonne. Then I put down my phone and take in my surroundings.

Parc Monceau is modeled after Victorian English gardens. It does not have the carefully pruned rows of trees present in the other *parcs*. Flora gently explodes here. There is beauty and magic in the contained disorder. There are few tourists here even when there are tourists, and even Parisians who don't live locally often don't seem all that familiar with it. Along the inner rim of the park runs a gravel path that is clogged with joggers. Handsome French men with rippling muscles. Taut women. Determined elderly. It's like the Reservoir in Central Park, but even more intense. I've come here to run on occasion, in years past, but mostly I like observing. I will bring a sandwich, find a bench, and watch lean figures whip by again and again. The shape of the benches along the path are sloped at an angle that forces you to recline. The chairs in the Lux are like this too; no sitting up straight here. No alertness. If posture dictates thought, thinking here should be detached too. It should languish. In the Lux and the Tuileries, the angle of chairs always strikes me as an amusing counterbalance to the formalities of the surrounding grounds.

All the benches in the shade at Monceau are taken today, so I set myself up on the grass.

Beside me lies an editing project I printed out before I left New York and have brought with the intention that I will spend my time here working on it, putting me in a position to pay my bills next year in 2022. I've been a freelancer for more than a decade now, and I've learned the hard way that having enough to live on for six months, as the financial experts love to advise, really means that you have enough to live on for four months; those last two months need to be spent setting up an income for the following six months. (The idea of saving beyond that largely remains just that, an idea.) Until this is accomplished, and I have enough in the bank to cover myself for that period of time, I find the anxiety drives everything else out. Financially, I'm currently good through Christmas, barring any sort of unforeseen event; a ludicrous rationale considering the relative unforeseenness of the last eighteen pandemic months in New York. But, as I've been reminded over and over again, I'm strangely suited to a world that mocks plans. It's been the unexpected payoff of choosing a life that so rarely allows for them. Over the years, I've realized that my "good" is often someone else's panicked emergency. In all these financial guides no one calculates one key thing: your individual risk tolerance. How hot must the water get before you—the frog—leap out? Even as I think this, I can hear the counterargument run in my head that it's easier to be risky when you don't have dependents (emotional and financial). And yes, obviously. But I counter it (to myself; spend as much time alone as I have, and "he said, she said" turns into an endless game of "me said, me said") by arguing that when you operate without a safety net, the inclination can be to ensure the tightrope is never strung too high. If there's no one there to catch you, common sense suggests you should stay close to the ground. That's never my inclination. Nina and I sometimes joke that we're going to write a *How to Live Well When You Have No Money* financial guide. In the end, it's less about having money than knowing what to do with the little money I have. This trip is costing me approximately $2,000, including airfare. Probably less, when you factor in that meals here are significantly cheaper than in New York, and my electricity bill won't be quadrupling thanks to my not being in New York to run my AC day and night.

Two thousand dollars is not nothing to me, but I also move through life in America with the knowledge that even if I had $2 million, one fall off my bike would result in my being truly bankrupt thanks to my terrible freelancer health insurance. Against this backdrop, it can be tough to conceive of $2,000 as being make-or-break, especially when it lands me here amidst all this lusciousness.

The savings account I'm really traveling on, the one that allows me to spend so little actual money, is the account made up entirely of relationships. I've been contributing to it slowly over the years, adding to it what I can when I can. An innocuous drink date that first summer, a trip to a concert the next. Casual afternoons at cafés. Concerts. Day trips out of the city. Weekends away. Until, one day, you realize you have a rich resource of relationships available to be tapped into. Goodwill. And concern. And shared joys and hardships. Something I often find all the more beautiful simply because it exists out of ritual. It is entirely self-created. It is voluntary. One shows up because one wants to.

I turn back to my work. I've studiously marked the pages of this editing project with a stack of colored Post-its, dividing the entire thing into sections that need to be tackled based on how many days I'm here. This is my new calendar. The current equation for my trip. The multicolored Post-its now flutter in the grass like strange flowers. Around me the park quietly undulates green. The lunch crowd is arriving, small groups with boxed lunches, wafts of cigarette smoke. It is still early August, the true *vacances* weeks, where everyone is off work, won't start till next week.

I put the manuscript on my lap with great determination. I am a disciplined person. Work will get done because it *must* get done. I read the opening paragraphs four or five times.

I return to my phone.

So far the difference between Fruitz and the other apps is that there is no pretense about why we are all on it. Despite the four different "fruit" categories, everyone is here for sex. Whatever fruit they've picked seems to be more a measure of whether they will say this immediately or after two exchanges. I'd been so struck by the Masseur asking me what I wanted, but quickly I've discovered that this is nearly everyone's first question. What am I looking for here? There is no preamble. And they don't mean it in the philosophical sense either. I've taken to responding to everyone the same. I'm here for enjoyment.

Which is the truth. But has also unexpectedly opened up a larger question for me. How do I intend to enjoy myself? What does enjoyment mean? What does it mean for me? Not just temporary enjoyment, like a massage. But as a thesis. How does one give themselves over to pleasure? How does a woman do so? It feels nearly impossible to separate myself from the pervasive voice of how women *should* be. As though I constantly live with an internal narrator who sometimes sounds like a book reviewer and sometimes like the voice of a women's magazine rack. But I think this is probably just the normal experience of moving through the world as a woman. And yet, how to quiet the internal monologue. The one that says: You are selfish. You are lucky. You are irresponsible. That despite feeling satisfied and fulfilled, you can't possibly be because you have opted out of the only satisfying and fulfilling things available to women (which no matter how much we profess to have progressed always seem to boil down to partners and parenting).

So far, aging often feels like an exercise in gaslighting. You might feel great. You might look great. And yet everyone and everything is telling you it's terrible. It's all terrible. Eventually every day becomes an endless decision to choose reality over consensus. I am feeling this, so it must be true versus everyone says this is true, so I will feel it too. The disconnect is so extreme at times, I find the result is I've come to distrust literally every story we've ever been told to expect as women, even when some of them have turned out to be true. To choose to enjoy things simply because they are enjoyable, even if no one quite believes you. To understand things are hard, even when you are constantly being told they are not *as* hard. This is true loneliness, I sometimes want to say. Because so much of enjoyment, and so much of bearing the hardest things, relies on the ability to do so with others. Misery loves company, but so does joy. And not the company of one other person. So many women in my life are told daily by their partner that they are beautiful, and yet move through the world feeling ugly. We need the company of a narrative.

I find that sometimes the easiest way to stick to your own experience of your life is, sadly, to stay quiet about it. Slide invisibly through the world doing exactly what you want. Don't offer anything up for review. If people don't know what you're doing, they can't tell you why it doesn't matter. Clearly this is not the route I have chosen, though I can see its appeal.

Still, I've taken Instagram off my phone, less for my own mental health than because I feel sensitive to how my life currently has the potential to make others feel bad. I don't want to be the person posting beach photos at the height of lockdown. I don't want to give the many women in my life, some of whom I know are currently disintegrating as they try to shoulder everyone else's needs, even more reason to feel terrible. I also don't want to spend my time here defending myself against the word *lucky*. Bad things happen to women because of something they've done, good things happen to us out of luck. I'm not here to fight that particular battle. I don't want to fight any battles. I don't actually want to do anything. But how does one do nothing?

Once, in my early thirties, when I was still working in book publishing as a foreign rights scout—my job was to read books on submission in America and let foreign publishers know whether they should bid on them—a hot British editor (hot as in career . . . this was publishing, after all) asked me why I didn't spend more time on the Upper East Side: "Go and find an older man to pay for you." We were eating steak at a back table at Raoul's, on our second martini. I was wearing my favorite black silk cocktail dress, which I now use as a shirt. I'd been in New York for ten years at that point, half spent as a waitress, which is to say, I understood he was trying to pay me a compliment. Publishing salaries were notoriously low, and he wanted me to know I still possessed the potential for more. It was still possible for me to hook a much bigger catch.

Why hadn't I? I have sometimes wondered this over the years, as I hang tight—a death hold, really—to a hard-won writing career while scraping together the bill payments from ever-decreasing word rates. Indeed, people, women mostly now, still suggest to me that in all likelihood my only route to real financial security, the kind that results in apartment ownership and not being bankrupted by health care, is to find a wealthy husband. "You could still do it," I'm assured, in the same tone one might use when encouraging a person to file an important application even though the deadline is just minutes away. I probably could, at least by the metric they are using, which I suspect mostly has to do with so-called good skin.

Even before we were all locked down into the most extreme versions of our life choices, I'd noticed this solution was gaining appeal in my friend set of women who had thus far always maintained—if not total, then enormous—self-sufficiency. There was an increased interest in stepping back and relinquishing control. These were the women who, as the popular, post-2016 march slogan says, are the granddaughters of the witches you couldn't burn. But the women are tired. No one cares how hard they are working. Independence is costly and risky, drudgery of a different sort. One solution people were toying with, if only in conversation (but isn't that always the first step), was to try on the idea, out of fashion long enough to feel radical, of letting the men pay. For everything.

"All I want to be is a lady who lunches" had, at least in my lunchtime conversations with unmarried women friends, replaced the corner office as a goal. I understood what my friends really meant, though. They wanted less work, less struggle, and more ease, stability, and comfort. Our culture promises us one direct path to that end. And it goes straight down an aisle and into a kitchen, where preferably, you are overseeing someone else doing the actual cooking.

But deep down, they also knew what I knew: that when it comes to getting married for money or security—both valid reasons!—you must give up the part where you get to do what you want. Not having to ask for anyone's permission, leaving on a whim, walking a high tightrope, is exhausting and scary, but once you're hooked on having control over your life, it's a hard drug to kick.

I return to Fruitz.

Another crush note about *tes yeux*. This one is forty-eight, tall and broad judging by the photos. Thick head of hair. Julien. He's just returned to Paris, his bio says, after years of living abroad. He speaks

English, French, and Serbian. He has sent me a question. *Café ou Vin?* I respond *Vin*.

And now there is another message from Masseur, who'd gone quiet after our first interaction.

"I would like to help you enjoy yourself," he writes for the second time. This had been his initial response to which I'd responded *bien*. That's where it had left off. "I will return to Paris at the end of the month. We will see each other then?" Following this are a series of numbers I assume are his WhatsApp contact info.

At this point there are at minimum thirty-five messages in this app alone—I ditched Bumble almost as quickly as I downloaded it; it requires too much work on my part to start the conversation. I want someone else to carry the bags for a while.

We've all spent the last year and more being allowed to want only the most basic things. To be healthy. To be safe. To not be punished all day every day for life choices made under a different set of rules. Being suddenly flung out of survival mode and into something else and being unsure of how to navigate feels like stepping off a boat and attempting to rediscover your land legs. The confidence will come after some strange lurching. Before I can say exactly what I want and where I want to go, I need to get comfortable with the fact I *can* want. I need to believe it, believe there is joy to be had and it is mine for the taking.

In Muriel Spark's novella *The Driver's Seat*, the narrator—a single, middle-aged (she's thirty-six) woman who lives in a small, intensely compact and organized flat—goes on holiday. Every step of the way her erratic behavior signals to us that her life exists outside the norm.

Her clashing clothes, her uncomfortable behavior on the plane that sends seatmates scurrying, her sharp interactions. Her difficultness. Bizarre behavior. She is unforgettable in the worst way. No wonder she's alone, the reader thinks. Who could tolerate this? Only at the end do we understand her behavior has been contrived to intentionally mark her movements, to *make* her visible, so that when she is murdered, it will be easy to retrace her steps. Only at the very last do we understand, this is not a woman at the mercy of a world she has not figured out or bothered to learn to navigate. This is a woman who was given a terminal health diagnosis and, instead of going quietly, has choreographed—quite spectacularly—her own demise. She will leave on her own terms. Loudly.

I'm currently not going quietly in quite the opposite direction. I'm attempting to contrive my own pleasure, without entirely understanding how I intend to get there. Let someone else do the driving for the moment. That's what I want. I want someone else to do the thinking.

I turn back to my phone. And type a message to Masseur.

"*Superbe,*" I write back and then switch to English. "How exactly do you plan to help me enjoy myself when you return?"

In the last few days this has become my approach as I ease into all these interactions. Like I am taking job applications: explain to me exactly what you have in mind should you get this role. It's been working wonders. After all these months craving touch, I'm the one who suddenly cannot stop feeling myself. It's as though there is a beast that slipped into me as I departed New York and is now rumbling around my body. In the movies this would be the basis of a horror story, a possession. The virus that spreads with increasing rapidity, resulting in a zombie apocalypse.

Perhaps the figure that most closely represents me right now is Sigourney Weaver's character in *Ghostbusters*. *After* she's been possessed by the presence of Zuul. There she is on the bed, writhing. Her hair askew, her makeup heavy now to insinuate the wild powers within that have been unleashed. Her dress hangs off her and she tugs it further asunder. Her teeth are practically vampirical. When Bill Murray tries to speak with her rationally—where is Dana, the civilized, disinterested woman he first encountered?—she levitates. She is otherworldly. Dangerous. And also a punch line. She wants to consume him.

I was not levitating off the bed. But I might have been. When I'm at home, I cannot get enough of myself. I seem unable to do anything other than consume myself with my own hands. Over and over and over again.

Despite my bajillion outfits, I had not thought to pack a vibrator. Nor do I need assistance from any of the easily accessible pornography hubs online. Whatever my fantasies were two years ago, they have, since March 2020, been narrowed down so severely that much like the image of the traveler dying of thirst in the desert forever reaching for the cool blue watery mirage, I have found my mind consumed with the desire for touch. For months all I had wanted to watch were naked massage videos. That was enough. The sight of someone being rubbed down seemed so exotic to me that even just glimpsing it felt electrifying.

Early on in lockdown I learned about a condition called skin hunger. It was first recognized in babies in orphanages in World War II and was diagnosed as "failure to thrive." In the famous Harry Harlow experiment, infant monkeys were removed from their mothers and given a choice between two inanimate surrogate mothers: one made out of wire and wood and the other made out of foam rubber and soft terry cloth. The wire mother had a milk bottle while the cloth mother did not. The infant monkeys' desire for touch and comfort was so strong it led them to choose the soft blanket mother every time, even over nourishment. Of our five senses—sight, smell, taste, sound, and touch—I was informed by Google that touch is the only one essential to human life.

I've never had to choose the sensation of touch over food, I eat constantly, but at one point during lockdown I began removing the vintage fur coats from my closet, despite the summer heat, and placing them across my bed or my couch so I could lay across them naked, like some Covid Burt Reynolds as the *Cosmo* centerfold, just to feel the sensation of another creature on my skin.

Now this creature currently inhabiting my body has fully taken over. My body feels amazing to me.

It feels amazing when I wake up, and again after coffee, and again after lunch. It feels amazing to return to myself *cinq à sept*. In Paris, *cinq à sept*, five to seven, is also slang for the after-work affair. It refers to the hours between leaving work and arriving home when one might theoretically take part in a sexual rendezvous. I have a suspicion this was more urban legend than reality. Or at least the reality was perhaps a brief time in the mid-twentieth century, pertaining only to a certain class, before women of that class fully entered the workforce. The years first captured simultaneously by film and television that had led us all to believe that these things had been occurring forever, were the way of things, were the *norm*.

Regardless, this is the frequency with which I feel compelled to storm my own body. Aided, at times, by the descriptions provided to me by strangers on my phone.

I return to the manuscript yet again. In addition to money, it represents my connection to practicality. I *should* be working on it. I know exactly what needs to be done and how to do it. But I don't want to. It's as simple as that. I don't want to work. Can I not work? Can I release myself from my own deeply embedded strict schedule that has enabled me to remain a freelancer this long? What will happen if I do?

I could at this moment lean on philosophy if I so chose. The last year and a half has everyone rethinking their schedules and what an optimized life really means. There's a seemingly endless amount of think pieces about how to get off the internet and do nothing. I have learned that the Latin word for business is *negotium*, which translates into the absence of leisure. The Romans (naturally) did not see leisure time as the slim reward for work, but work as a negative space defined by leisure.

Or I could stick with the French. At one point so many pieces had linked back to Cuban-born French (naturally) philosopher Paul Lafargue's 1883 treatise *The Right to be Lazy* it was open on three different tabs on my computer screen (I am lazy about closing tabs if nothing else). Lafargue argued that the eight-hour workday was servitude, and the labor movement should be fighting to work even less.

Or I could lean on Audre Lorde, who argued that the erotic is where a woman's true power lies (not to be confused with the pornographic). "It is an internal sense of satisfaction to which, once we have experienced it, we know we can aspire. For having experienced the fullness of this depth of feeling and recognizing its power, in honor and self-respect we can require no less of ourselves."

A generous observer might suggest that what I am cultivating is some combination of these three intensely serious lines of thought. I do feel surprisingly powerful. But the truth is, I simply do not want to do anything that does not bring me enjoyment. And as there is no one to make me do otherwise, I succumb to myself and decide to heed the lyrics of that timeless tune, and give myself over to absolute pleasure. Whatever it looks like. However it arrives.

I shove the manuscript back in my tote bag. When I get home, a few hours later, I slide it into the back pocket of my suitcase. Goodbye to all that.

At least for this month.

And then I lie down on the bed and reopen Fruitz to find out all the new ways the people there intend to bring me pleasure.

SEVEN

On Va Prendre

The first week in Paris is filled with carafes of wine and friends. *Même, s'il vous plaît. Une autre, s'il vous plaît.* One morning (a loose term, shortly after I wake up, the church bell rings twelve times) I message the group saying the only thing that will solve the state of my rosé-saturated body is the sort of greasy diner brunch breakfast it's impossible to find in Paris. Or so I thought. Sandra responds that there's a newish place up in the 18th around the corner from Sacré Coeur. It's run by Australians and has an incredible brunch.

"Actual brunch?" I ask.

"Yes! And *chocolat chaud* with huge chunks of chocolate."

The thrill of someone hearing you and acting on it.

This becomes our weekend plan.

We will get there at 15h00. They stop serving at 15h30.

. . .

How did I acquire this friend group? I get asked this sometimes, not just about Paris, but in general. But who are they? How? As though I am leading a secret double life. The truth is, I'm leading a number of lives, none of them particularly secret. But something about building quality friendships later in life seems to fascinate. Which has always puzzled me. The older I get, the better I know myself, the less distance I must travel to figure out whether to include someone in my life. The closer I am to me, the closer I am to other people (and conversely, the less time I need to figure out whether to keep them at arm's length).

Still, I've realized a lot of people seem to establish their friends in college (high school, even) and this group is who they end up riding through life with. Many of my friendships are also decades long (including from high school). Some span more than half my life at this point, a fact I'm equal parts grateful for and proud of. But when so many people simultaneously veered off into marriages and children, the sense that I needed to broaden the base, add more legs to the table, became painfully clear. Much the same way, I imagine, the first person to have a child in any group needs to find support elsewhere or they sink. It was during these years—when many of my friends took the road to partners and parenthood—that I began to travel more. My job—or *jobs*, as is always the case when you're a freelancer— allowed me to work from anywhere. And I did. Instead of weeklong vacations I'd go for weeks at a time. I'd attempt to live instead of just visit. In this way, my life allowed me to establish multiple lives. Little bubbles of routines in other places. I'd say yes to every "you should meet this person." I would always get the contact info of new people at the table and follow up. I began to view every person I was introduced to as a potential root in a new location. A source of information and help so that I could return, people who, if nothing else, might hear about apartments available for long-term stays, for instance. All of this, so that when I did return I would not be starting from scratch. I would have options.

When I think of my years in Paris, and how I went from the early days of near-complete solitude to the soft landing I have now, I'm reminded, somewhat hysterically, of that graph they showed us in health class in the eighties to explain how STDs spread. She sleeps with one person, and then they sleep with one person and so on until everyone is infected. An imperfect analogy to be sure. But there is some truth to it: I just tried to remain as open as possible and say yes to everyone. Some clicked. Some fit immediately. I stayed in touch. And then the next year more, and then the year after that more. Until this many years later I have a rich established life here that lets me call Paris, if not home exactly, then homelike.

I arrive at brunch a puddle of sweat. Aarti and Sandra and Ellie are already in line. Nina is on deadline for something and can't come. The irony of an empty city and yet still we wait. There is only outdoor seating, of course. Tables squeezed together on the street under a slanted roof, the same as the ones in New York. Half the line is masked. A young, heavyset woman at the door in a fuchsia tank is taking names. A burly masked man with short, cropped hair and colorful heavily tattooed arms is moving to and fro, taking orders, delivering food, dropping checks. I can hear his Australian accent when he stops to describe dishes. It feels like brunch in Brooklyn.

We are all hungry. Starving. The line is not moving. There appears to be a table for four that is sitting empty. We are definitely going to order the *pain perdu*. We must have the *pain perdu*. Why is that table still empty? Does she see that the table is still empty? That other table has had the card on their check for like five minutes. I am starving. Just wait till you try the *chocolat chaud*. Our conversation is comforting in its utter mundaneness.

Nailed into the wall we are leaning against is a plaque marking the spot where a person named Simone was assassinated by the Gestapo. There are still a few dried flowers wedged into the corner from Bastille Day. There are plaques like these all around Paris.

I tap the plaque.

"We might be hungry, but at least we're not being assassinated by the Gestapo."

Everyone looks at it for the first time.

"True," Ellie says after a moment. "Puts things in perspective."

We move forward.

The table for four is still free.

Finally, we sit.

The menu is so thick with butter and sugar and fat it feels like a photo that is slow to load and come into focus. I have to stare at it for a while. Words like *Pork Belly, Duck Confit, Lobster Benedict, Salmon*

Millefeuille, Champignon, Fried Brioche, Honey and Cinnamon Fromage Blanc, Eggs Cocotte (it sounds like they are flashing some leg). This, I think, is why the French are so strict with language and behavior (and for a long time, dress). They must counterbalance the excess of the butter and the skin and the sex.

The burly Australian with the tattoos comes over to take our order. Our masks go back up. He has very blue eyes that seem to connect with mine like two magnets meeting. Oh that jolt. I haven't had a jolt like that for a long time. That sense of hurtling over all the small talk. On the apps it's an act of faith. A guessing game and a roll of the dice. In real life it just is or it isn't. Part of the charge I'm feeling is just remembering the sensation of real-life connection with a stranger. No time to pick everything apart. Just curiosity based on some sort of animal instinct.

He goes around the table answering everyone's "Should I order this or that, which do you prefer?" questions. Sandra asks what sixty-four-degree eggs means. While he's explaining it—something to do with how it's cooked that goes entirely over my head—he only looks at me. That is, until he spots Marcel, Sandra's dog, who is calmly asleep under her chair. And then he does that thing dog owners do, and immediately launches into a monologue about his own dog. Like Marcel, *his* dog is also a rescue. His dog also lives in Montmartre and has his own Instagram account. Unlike Marcel, who is a constant ball of love and affection, his dog is afraid of people and sometimes snaps.

He continues to only look at me as he's saying this. He has that aggressive chef energy that comes with living in a world where the law of the land is the temperature of the skillet and dominated by the primal desire of taste. Combined with the directness of an Australian minus the good mood (which might just have been beaten out of him by the brunch crowd). Now he's raging about the people who are unmasked. About the people who complained about curfew. He hasn't been able to get home. He's an opera of tattoos. I want to know what it's like to be cooked for by him. This is going nowhere—he's already mentioned that his partner is home with the dog—but even innocent crushes are so fun, and somehow reassuring. I am alive in the world.

I order the burrata with the sixty-four-degree eggs and thick slices of bacon, bread with jam and butter, and a bowl size of *chocolat chaud* that comes with a chunk of chocolate in the cup and a small jug full of *chocolat chaud* on the side. We order *pain perdu* to share. I tell Sandra I will take the extra bacon she does not want in her mushroom scramble with *chèvre* and hazelnut crumble and olive bread. I tell Ellie I will absolutely have some of her special pancakes with *cerises fraîches*. And then we wait.

Immediately the conversation goes where it always does. To numbers.

Sandra hates her apartment. From a distance it is picture perfect. A Montmartre flat. A picturesque view. But in the living, it faces onto a square and every afternoon musicians set up there and play late into the night. These days, even without the tourists, they are still there. Around midnight it turns into some sort of party and Sandra is kept awake until the early hours by the sound of bottles being smashed on the cobblestone. In the morning she has to carry Marcel a few blocks until it's safe for him to walk.

"I miss lockdown," she says. "There were a few months where it felt like the neighborhood came together and you could figure out who actually lived there." She pauses. "And at least I could sleep."

"Why don't you move?"

"I can't afford it."

I think of this generation of career media people who got on the roller coaster back in the late nineties when the ride looked like a steep one to the top, at which point you'd get the office and the title and then be propelled onward by a great swoosh of expense accounts and town cars and underwritten mortgages all the way through to the end of a respected career. Instead, by the time the ride we were on got to the top, the rails ran out and now everyone is just hanging on by their thumbs waiting for some structure to appear, but it never does. I still make the same word rate, or less, than I did when I started out, while every other expense has quadrupled.

"Didn't rent prices fall here too?" I ask. New York had been so abandoned I'd managed to get my rent *lowered* by $200 a month. Unheard of.

"It doesn't matter."

I recognize that tone. It's the tone of a savings account that is close to being emptied with no sure prospect of being refilled. I fill in the space.

"I will never get over not having a down payment to take advantage of those six weeks last spring when everyone really ran for it," I say.

And this immediately opens the door to what has become the eternal math equation. If my thirties were all about calculating marriage and fertility, my forties are all about calculating down payments. Mortgages. And, because I live in New York, maintenance fees. The monthly fee you pay on top of your mortgage to the building to maintain it. In Manhattan co-ops this number is often the equivalent of rent, which means by buying, you are doubling your monthly payment, one half of which will continue in perpetuity. And then there are health

insurance premiums. It's all part of the larger question: How to remain in the partnership I've struck with a city instead of a person?
Some of my most enjoyable conversations in Paris involve my explaining
this financial torture device, along with health insurance deductibles,
to European dinner companions if only because the looks of horror I
elicit somehow placate me. It really *is* that awful, they say.

"Could you have bought?" asks Ellie. As though we are talking
about a computer or even a car. Something in the realm of practical
reality.

"Probably not as a freelancer," I say. "I'd need to show consistent
pay stubs and savings in my bank account to pass the co-op board interview. Then with the maintenance plus the mortgage, I'd be paying
nearly $5K a month. But I like to *think* about it."

"$5K a month for what?!"

"My 450-square-foot studio."

And we're off. Ellie paid €230,000 for her three-hundred-square-
foot apartment just outside the Périph two years ago. No down payment required.

"None?!"

"No. I have a CDI and as a first-time buyer they give you that
option."

A CDI is basically a guarantee when you sign the contract to be
hired full time that you can't get fired. There are no credit cards in
France. Not as Americans understand them.

Ellie is on the fence about selling her place. She wants something
bigger and will go farther out, but the drop in prices is hitting her as
a seller.

Sandra looks deflated. "I'll never be able to buy."

Aarti pays €1,000 a month for her one-bedroom in the 11th. She's on the hunt for a place to purchase; as a foreign hire who was scouted here by her company she's eligible for a tax reduction of some sort. But she's waiting to see if her boyfriend will go in on it with her.

"The only way an apartment purchase will work for me is if I can do an all-cash purchase," I say.

"How much would that be?" asks Ellie with the natural-born face of a problem solver.

"I'd say a million."

"A million?!"

"At least." I break it down: "I'd need $800,000 to purchase. Then the remainder to cover fees and repairs. If it was a co-op I'd need twice that to show I have enough in the bank to cover the monthly expenses."

"That is absolutely fucking insane."

"So $2 million?" says Aarti, wide-eyed.

"Yes, $2 million would solve a lot of things for me."

In New York, I find, we all—*we* being women without outside support of partner or family—have our number. There's an episode of *Sex and the City* (is there a way to age as a woman without thinking of some episode of that show?) where Miranda says her "scary age" is forty-three and Carrie says hers is forty-five. They are both in their late thirties and they're talking babies and marriage (what else). Having hurtled past both those numbers, I've come to think of my forties as the age where the mortgage math takes over. What is the number that will make it possible to get the tests the doctor orders without having to worry about bankruptcy? What is the number that means you don't approach every rent renewal wondering if the $10,000 you've finally scrounged together for savings will be spent on a broker's fee and down payment looking for a new apartment? What is the number that will make it okay that there is no one to ask for help? What is the number that spells a modicum of safety?

For me, that number is $2 million.

I'm lowballing my number, according to my friends in New York. They all say $5 million. But my number is based on the practical expectation that I will keep working. Somehow having an actual number makes it more plausible to me. A concrete destination. The possibility of my ever coming into $2 million is slim to never. And yet, the distance also brings me a perverse comfort: How can I possibly expect security when I'm this far away from it? Still, I think, should it ever happen, I will know what to do with it.

Of course, I could get a full-time job. Become a copywriter for a corporation. Take the benefits. And the two weeks of vacation a year. But I won't. That there is no longer a way to make a reasonable living doing the thing I'm good at is not yet enough to entice me away from the cliff's edge I walk.

We talk of cities these days the way we used to talk about partners. How do we get them to commit? How do we convince them to let us stay permanently? Satisfy us emotionally and financially. To want us. To give us a safe haven. Of course, there is no guarantee a partner will give you this either. They could suck you dry too. I have watched it happen again and again. Forget bicoastal, I want to say. I'm in a throuple with Paris and New York.

I often feel I can only understand discussions about long-term relationships in terms of cities: What I love, what I loathe, and what I'm willing to tolerate because it's better than anywhere else. And how, after such a long time, it's sometimes the history that keeps you coming back. I wonder sometimes if I even see New York as it is these days or if I'm walking around in a city that now only exists in my head. Before lockdown, I was spending less and less time there. I'd been with New York for nearly a quarter of a century, but the longer I'm there the more impossible it becomes for me to love it unless I'm away from it for long periods of time. It's always waiting for me when I come back. But without Paris it's no longer enough. Like married couples who, once the kids have left, spend more time at greater distances. Remaining together by remaining apart for longer stretches.

Finally, we finish eating. The sky has become overcast. Everyone has a different place they want to be. Aarti is going up to the flea. Sandra home to wait for a delivery.

"I think I will *en Vélib'*," I say.

Ellie guffaws at my butchered French. *"En Vélib'!"*

"I'm a Vélib'er, I couldn't leave her if I tried," I sing to the tune of the old Monkees song.

More laughs.

"Fine, I will too, then," says Ellie.

"Do you bike?" I ask.

"Of course."

Over brunch Ellie had mentioned someone she'd connected with on one of the apps. He is a *pompier* (firefighter). She saw a photo of him lifting weights at the firehouse and said, "Yes please."

"I'm not sure I'd want anyone to see me naked at this point," says Sandra, feeding Marcel, who is now on her lap, bits of croissant.

"Oh well, he'll get what he gets, and he'll like it" is Ellie's reply.

In the short time we've known each other, I've come to think this

97

is Ellie's approach to most people. She is a strong dose of life. Unfiltered. We are all—me, Nina, Sandra, Aarti—a strong dose in our own ways, but Ellie leads with it as though there is a flag perpetually raised in her hand as she storms the world. I'd eventually come to learn she'd been in Paris for eight years. An engagement had ended when her fiancé died. She was a live translator for a mostly male tech company. The five languages she spoke, in addition to French, she learned as an adult. The trick, she tells me, is to watch foreign films and put the subtitles on in the language the actors are actually speaking. Even in the short amount of time we've spent together, more than a few Parisians have reflected on her lack of accent when she speaks French.

I tell Ellie I'll go with her to the Vélib' stand. Assuming we'll go our separate ways once we get there. She says there's one below the Sacré Coeur at the Métro.

Aarti shakes her head. "I could just never do it. It's insane, the Vélib'."

"I love it," I say.

"It's the only way," says Ellie.

Liberator

here is really only one person who I would consider biking around a city with: my friend Maddy. A native New Yorker, she gave me my first New York bike not long after September 11, when taking the train proved too wearing on the nerves. We'd ride into our waitressing shift in Greenwich Village through 5:00 p.m. rush hour traffic, and then home again at 5:00 a.m. through the empty downtown canyons.

Biking in a city has almost nothing to do with understanding—or even necessarily liking—bikes. You couldn't pay me to go on some sort of biking travel tour in, say, the Loire. Or to casually roll down a leisurely city bike path along a river. Instead, it has everything to do with understanding, and respecting, the city you are biking. It requires you to pay attention. To everything. To want to fly up and down the city's arteries, zip across from limb to limb. To be willing to be extremely alive. As I wrote once about biking New York, "To know a city by bike is to know it intimately in a way not possible by foot or car . . . like being thrust into the bloodstream of a great beast, privy to its every pulse . . . you learn the beats and melody of the streets the way you learn any song."

To immediately understand the mood of its day.

It's a shortcut into the daily human condition. And it can be a drug.

To do that with another person requires a particular intimacy and trust that's not easy to come by.

Ellie and I drop Aarti off at the Métro, and then I follow Ellie around the corner to a long stand of Vélib's. She is peering at her phone.

"We don't really need an electric, do we? It's all downhill from here. Number seventeen is good." She taps the seat, still looking at her phone. "Number eleven." Hand shoots to further down the line. "Oh! Number thirty-three, take that!"

I'm already standing beside the bike whose seat is the highest. I have no idea what she's talking about.

"What do you mean?"

"On the app. They're all rated." She is testing the pedals and tapping the wheels of a bike as she says this. Like a practiced mechanic.

I look at the app. I notice, for the first time, all the bikes are rated by stars. Three is the best. It also lets you know how recently they've been rated. The one I'm standing beside has one star. I move to thirty-three.

Off we go.

I know the basics of Paris on a bike. The main boulevards. I no longer need to stop and start and check my maps. I've also learned the hard way not to take shortcuts. Not to assume that when I get to one of the large places, the huge roundabouts that have multiple roads shooting off them, that I can guess which one to take. One innocent left-hand turn on your way to the 8th, one exit too early—only fifteen feet between this corner and that!—and suddenly you find yourself in the 20th. But Ellie knows the roads. Soon we are flying. Into the bowels of the city. Down narrow streets where the even narrower bike lanes run against the direction of traffic. Sailing through intersections. Paris has slipped into the August slowdown, but there are still plenty of cars on the road. I've never been good with the traffic lights here. I find them small, and strangely placed off to the side. I'm never sure where to look for them. But Ellie is not slowing down. It's keep up or go your own way. I want to learn to bike the city like this. This is the Parisian fluency I'm after.

I take the intersections on faith that Ellie knows what she's doing. Her right arm shoots out to indicate we're turning right. We swing out onto a large boulevard, merging with the traffic. Don't blink, I think. This is one of those instances where you have to commit and not second-guess. I do and I don't. We cross four lanes of cars and line up with the traffic to make a left onto a wide, sweeping roundabout. I have only the vaguest sense of where we are now. I keep my eyes focused on Ellie. She's in a short flowery dress (which I've come to recognize as her staple look), her long blonde hair untied, wearing white sneakers. The light changes and onto the roundabout we go. I'm about fifteen feet behind her and I watch the cars slow for her as they take in the blonde hair and the long tan legs. Bike or no bike, she is an entire language that demands right of way. Her right arm shoots out again to signal our exit.

To my amazement the cars really defer to bikes as though we have a right to be on the road. I love this formality. In New York, you're liable to get run down, indication or not. *You* must defer to traffic. Not here. Here we have a right to the road.

I can hear Ellie's voice above the traffic, repeating the joke I made earlier.

"I'm a Vélib'er, I couldn't leave her if I tried."

I burst out laughing. If I could throw my arms up in celebration, I would. But these bikes are at least fifteen pounds and my balance is not what it once was. But it is hard to think of another way to express the joy of finding a person who is made to feel the most alive by the very thing that makes you feel most alive. It is one of the great gifts. One that transcends even language. Or is its own language. The gift of not having to translate yourself.

At the next major intersection Ellie stops even though the light is green, and turns back to look at me for the first time since we set off.

"You go left here." She points down the wide boulevard.

I look around and realize we're at Rivoli, and ahead of us is the Louvre.

"Which way do you go?"

"Straight across."

The lights change and she's off, disappearing across Rivoli and through the arch. I make a left and head home. It's a straight shot from here.

EIGHT

Skin Hunger

Everyone on Fruitz is interested in spanking me.

At least this is how it feels when I dive into my messages.

It's not the first thing they tell me. Though I'm realizing at the bottom of many of the profiles there are often a series of letters, and I've started to wonder whether they signify something I should be aware of.

I ask Ellie what MMM means.

"Oh, it's one of those bullshit things, like sapiosexual. They basically just want you to know they'll go down on you. Orgasms as Olympic sport."

"Mine or theirs?"

"Yours. The French take female pleasure seriously. Getting women off makes them feel like men."

"Excellent! But then what is sapiosexual?"

"It means they're turned on by your mind."

"Is that a real thing?"

"No."

Exactly nothing about my mind is on display right now, beyond the fact I don't want to use it. My messages, however, have gone from *Penthouse Letters* to full erotica. They contain, if not entire novels, long descriptive passages that need only be loosely stitched together by the briefest of plotlines to be made a narrative. Shades of Fruitz.

This is of my own doing. I've begun pressing for more details. Like anything else that feels good, I want more. The initial rush of so much attention has, if not exactly worn off, simply made me want to maintain it, which means I need to turn it up a notch. After a week of swiping I'm now more surprised when people *don't* immediately match with me. When I open the app and don't find four or five crush notes waiting for me, I will close and restart it assuming the issue is that the app hasn't refreshed, not that the crush notes have run out. I'm usually right.

That the notes are almost always the same—some variation on *tes yeux, les cheveux*—hasn't yet lost its allure, but I understand that if I want to get to the next level, I'm going to have to be the one to make it possible. Now, even if they don't ask me what I'm looking for here, I respond to their initial volley by telling them I'm *très bien* and I'm here to enjoy myself. The shift to English is notable, and I'm asked if I prefer it. I'm stronger in English, I say. Which is both true, and also saves me the delay in having to plug everything into Google Translate, to make sure I'm understanding correctly, and then wait for my international plan to load the result.

"I'd like to help you enjoy yourself."

"Wonderful, how so?"

"I'd like to give you pleasure."

"What will you do, do you think?" I write back.

And we're off to the races. No one has yet asked me what I, if any-thing, plan to do in return. Which, for right now, is ideal. I am here to receive.

The first time I do this, I immediately put my phone down, the way Carrie Bradshaw ducked below her desk the first time Aidan sent her an AIM message (who could have guessed how innocent so much of that show would someday seem), unable to attach myself to the au-dacity of being so direct with my own wants. But then the responses come pouring in. And I like it.

"If you come to my home? I think I will kiss you and put my hand under your skirt. If you are agreed of course."

"What else," I type back, surprised at my ability to demand more.

"After, it depends of your desires: do you want to be tighted, blindfolded . . . But I will use my tongue and my fingers."

I smile at the clunky translation. I wonder how my desires would read if I attempted French without any sort of Google translation. I tell Blindfold this sounds nice, then I move on to the next message.

It's not just that I've landed in Paris somewhat frenzied for touch that makes these descriptions appealing and not intrusive or . . . objectifying. They don't leave me feeling . . . I struggle to think of the word . . . used, I suppose. And it's not just that I'm on holiday; Paris has ceased to feel like a vacation destination and is now more of a second life I return to when I can. Nor is it that I am, very literally, asking for it.

It's that some element of consent weaves its way through nearly every message I receive. Descriptions are almost always followed by the question, would I enjoy that?

As pleasurable as some of the details strike me, there is also the intense pleasure of asking someone to not just put thought into me, but go the extra distance to articulate it. Literally write it down, step by step. Show and tell. Perhaps what I'm really asking for is to be courted, pornographically, by strangers. To be seen.

Even the ones declaring, quite abruptly, their interest in "licking" me don't entirely throw me off. The directness of this phrase is both amusing and off-putting, though its frequency eventually makes me think it's a hiccup of French translation. Of course, I have no idea if the people on the other end are simply putting their French through the same Google translation I'm using. Ellie tells me she doesn't worry about the future of her job as a live translator because good translation is more than a literal conversion of words; it's understanding the *meaning* and being able to articulate that. The French famously refer to the orgasm as *la petite mort.* But less well known is the French phrase (or one of them) for cunnilingus (leave it to the English language to make a pleasurable experience sound like a trip to the gynecologist): *brouter le cresson*, which literally translates into grazing the watercress. When you think about it, solid description.

There is very little translation needed for what I am after, and yet the language of, if not love, then physicality, is powerful. I start to cut off the ones who only give me a line or two, seemingly by rote, as though copying and pasting the description of a Pornhub video (which might be the case!). I keep the ones who ask me if I'd prefer they do this or this. Would it be okay if they did that or that. Sometimes I say yes just to see where they will go next. Like an X-rated choose your own adventure. This is where it almost always veers into spanking. Spanking starts to feel like the Fruitz version of men who like to post photos of themselves with animals to their dating profile.

It goes the other way too. My "what elses" inevitably open the door to men who want to tell me more about themselves.

My wife divorced me and my girlfriend wants to open our relationship.

I have three children and could really use this break.

My wife wants us to see other people.

My wife is no longer interested in me.

I read these messages and feel that muscle, the one that's been trained all my life to lend a sympathetic ear, twitch. But that is not what I'm here for. No thank you. I have spent a year being the sympathetic ear for people I know and love who, if it will ever be possible again, regularly feed me. I will not be doing it now. Not for strangers. Nope. Goodbye.

I don't actually say goodbye, I simply unmatch. I feel rather brutal about it the first time I do it. But when I tell Ellie about the man who has quickly moved on from expressing admiration over my hair to telling me he needs help understanding why his ex-girlfriend suddenly lost interest, she shows no mercy.

"I think fucking not," she says. "Unmatch."

"It feels mean."

"Online dating is a contact sport. Don't go in if you can't handle it. You're not a fucking therapist."

I had to stop going to a therapist a month or so into the first lock-down because she cost $300 a session and it was unclear where my money would be coming from for the next while.

"Maybe I should tell them I will listen for $300 an hour."

"God, do you think it would be worth it?"

Good point. I unmatch.

It gets easier after the first time.

I immediately cancel out everyone who tells me they're in an open relationship unless they have posted a photo of their actual partner in their profile. In my experience open relationships almost always describe one person's desires and another person's acquiescence or ignorance. No thank you.

Same goes for the ones who use their wedding photo to say they are looking for company. I don't fault the ask, but the lack of sense. Can you not find another photo? It spells messiness to me.

Then there are the fake profiles. They stand out almost immediately. The too-good-looking doctor who messages a long paragraph to tell me how pleased he is to meet me, he is a surgeon in Canada, which is not a problem because of technology and plane tickets. Why don't we switch to email so we can really get to know each other. It's the Tinder version of the Nigerian bank account scam.

I tell Ellie I'm bummed that one man I was chatting with, who seemed interesting, had abruptly disappeared.

"It doesn't matter," she says firmly. "Just keep swiping. There's always more."

This, more than the crush notes, more than the messages that sometimes send me back to my own body, is what I am enjoying the most. The abundance. There really is always more. I am released from the trap of gratefulness. I have been relinquished from the scarcity mind-set that drives . . . basically all things women, I suppose.

I've moved into an abundance mind-set. I'm Instagram therapy-speak made real. The fact I've kept Instagram off my phone may have something to do with it. It's easier to experience abundance when you aren't being bombarded with images of everyone else's.

This mind-set slides into everything. I buy salted butter from the Marché Bastille and make my eggs with it in the morning, dropping huge squares into the frying pan so that the eggs turn crisp and brown on the outside almost as if I'm deep-frying them. I slather it on my daily baguette in thick squares and then add equally thick squares of Lindt Lait Praliné Feuilleté chocolate on top. I start to gauge the schedule of the *boulangerie* and make a point to stop by at 15h00 in the hopes of increasing my chances of getting a warm *pain au chocolat*. When I do, the pastry is still gooey with butter, soft and melting instead of crisp and flaky, and the bars of chocolate baked inside ooze out across my fingers, sometimes leaving streaks of chocolate around my mouth. Every morning I take a shower, pruning myself the way I imagine gardeners attend to their gardens, and then slather cream over every inch of my body, followed by oils and then more oils. My body feels like a velvet glove. I become aware of the sensation of air on the backs of my knees, my belly, the skin between my toes. The expectation of others seeing my body leads me to see it anew. To enjoy it anew.

The contact I've been after, however, has yet to actually materialize. This is almost entirely my own doing. I keep canceling dates.

In part, this is because once out with my friends I find it difficult to pull myself away to an experience that, while appealing, is not guaranteed. My skin might be starving, but no more than my brain or, I suppose, my soul is for communion. I find myself out in the evenings, in the midst of conversation, hands sliding across the table for this meat or that cheese, or the hard end of the baguette, or to dole out the last of the carafe of rosé—*une autre s'il vous plaît*—and lean back into the conversation as though into a wave that carries me along, gently and securely. But also with direction and determination. *To be understood.* To be celebrated for things you do not have to explain. To be together. What kind of sex can compete with this? Not the unknown kind.

And so, for the first week or so, my messages are littered with *désolée* (if you're going to cancel at the last minute, at least do it in the language of the person you're canceling on) and perhaps another time?

Sometimes I find the person has unmatched. There is a twenty-two-year-old in Belleville who wants me to come to some sort of swingers party. He is handsome and taut and his messages are charming. But the wine is flowing, and the conversation is flowing, and I don't want out of this. When I look a little later he has disappeared from my messages entirely. Profile deleted. So too goes the Canadian who has been waiting for two days for me to confirm a time and place. I had told him earlier, after 23h00? But now it is nearly midnight, and we've just ordered another pizza, and another carafe, and why would I leave this?

"Just keep swiping," says Ellie.

But there's more at work here than just preferring friendship. It's the same way you can't expect to run a marathon after not exercising for a year. I recognize I need to work up to this real-life sex. This is one of the reasons the messages have been so appealing. It feels like a warm-up. I know the game I want my head and body to be in, I'm just not there yet. But I'm getting closer every day.

The man I've begun to call Le Spanker hangs in there, though when I glance at his profile I realize his distance from me is steadily increasing. *Les vacances* have started.

His initial question to me had been "Pop corn *sucré ou salé?*" I answered *salé*. He responded: "Good answer. It was also something like, Do you like it more sweetly or sweaty? :)"

And then twenty minutes later:

"Dammit. It seems that each time I look you're farther away."

"Which one of us is on a train?" I write back.

He tells me he's traveling from Poitiers to Montpellier. I respond with three wave emojis.

"What does it mean? The ocean instead of the sea?"

And then, before I can respond: "I hope I don't waste your time by texting too much. I try sexting but you didn't catch it."

The awareness he might be wasting my time strikes me as considerate.

"You're not wasting my time," I say. "And you're right, I didn't catch it."

This is not true. I get the salty and the sweet and the sweaty. But let him tell me.

Instead, he says, "Good to know. Well, you're forgiven because it was subtle/hidden. I like talking with several meanings. It was a parallel between sugar and salt, sweety and sweaty, gentle and wild."

I recognize that at any other time in pre-times the "you're forgiven" would have left me cold. But I'm actually enjoying the fact this conversation has not immediately transitioned into the sex maneuvers.

"Makes sense now," I write. And then, "Thank you for forgiving me." I leave off the emoji that would make it clear whether or not I am being sarcastic. I find this all amusing, and I'm curious where it might go.

"Well, I'm like that. I can forgive you if you deserve it but I can also punish when you deserve it." Followed by a fire and a devil emoji. "It's on you but we're not here. Yet."

Ah, that consent.

I can feel all these questions and comments and descriptions working their way through me like a glass of wine, changing the way I move, and how I see things. How I see myself, yes. But also, how I see others. The calculations that have been running in my head for years about appropriateness, or faults, or warning signs are nowhere to be found. Everyone has an appeal. Every movement, turn of head, arm gesture, gait of walk is simply an advertisement for how that person is likely to behave in bed. I wonder if this is what it's like to move through the world like a man. People I pass on the street; the ones who sell me my daily baguette; the *gendarmes* who are always leaving the Lux in the morning when I enter to run. Everyone has become an invitation. I've stopped worrying about the dates I am canceling and just let myself go where I please, assuming it will just be a matter of time before I answer the call.

On Saturday Nina, Sandra, Aarti, Ellie, and I plan a picnic on the Seine.

I meet Nina at the corner and we walk down Rue de la Roquette together. There was a time in the late nineties where I lived within walking distance of most of my friends, before we scattered to different parts of the city based on relationships and finances. I'm reminded of the enormous, shared comfort of that. Community as the everyday.

It's a nice walk. The early evening spread out against the sky. The absence of noisy late drinkers has made the street less loathsome this year. In normal times this stretch of Rue de la Roquette draws hordes of the under-thirty set who on the weekends rage from midafternoon late into the night. Without them I no longer feel as though I'm living in the midst of some terrible version of Paris constructed by a fraternity house. I recognize the irony of loving a city more when there are fewer people, the very thing that makes it a city. But in the last year it's been the chorus of everyone I know who lives in a place that is often overrun with visitors. Like the evening after the houseguests have left, it's a relief.

Nina has brought with her the prosciutto and a baguette. I pop into the *boulangerie* on the corner, the one that never corrects my French by immediately repeating back to me my order, and get two more, still warm from the oven. We need cheese now and rosé. Because so much of Paris is closed in August, the month I am most frequently here, I've become more familiar with the grocery store chains than I might otherwise have if I knew the Paris that fires on all cylinders. For instance, when it comes to cheese, I only know the *fromage* aisle at the Franprix. Initially this felt like a defeat—why come to Paris if not to bask in the wonder of their *fromageries?* But they're almost all *en vacances,* leaving me no choice. It took a few summers for me to realize that shopping at the Franprix, or the Carrefour, or even Monoprix, is probably one of the more normal Parisian things I do.

This is where we are headed now. There is a Franprix at the bottom of Boulevard Henri IV just before you cross over to the river. It's one of the few in the city that is open late and also on Sundays, and every time I'm in there something about the bad lighting and general disarray reminds me of the Lower East Side bodegas of my late-nineties New York. It also has a better selection than any artisanal cheese and wineshop in Manhattan. It is packed with people when we arrive. Apparently everyone has the same plans we do.

We all have our assignments. Sandra is bringing burrata and hummus. Ellie has watermelon and Saint Félicien. Aarti has champagne from her trip to the region the other week and also cucumbers. We buy olives, baby carrots, some Roquefort in a plastic wedge container, a circle of *chèvre* wrapped in paper, and a soft strong cheese I discovered a few days earlier, but recognize only by the packaging. Each costs no more than three euros. I stop at the fridge and pull out three bottles of rosé, all Côtes du Rhône, five euros each. It's ridiculous to say there is no bad wine in France, but I feel confident saying there is less. And it's rare enough I don't worry about encountering it. We get in line for the auto checkout; I see them everywhere now and for some reason they strike me as very un-French; you still have to pull a lever to get a paper Métro ticket here, after all. That said, I prefer them because they have language options: English, German, and Spanish. I refuse to hit English, even on my first days here; I don't want a recorded voice blurting out my touristness. Instead, I muddle my way through the French prompts and consider it a small language lesson.

This sometimes gets me in trouble when I have to weigh individual fruit and don't entirely understand what it's telling me to do; the surprised look of the clerk who comes over to explain and realizes I'm not French never fails to make me cringe.

Tonight, there are long lines for all the checkouts. Cheese and rosé and chips are moving in a steady flow out the door. Soon, we too are streaming down to the river. Past the ancient-looking building on the corner with its fierce bearded men carved in stone. Across Quai des Célestins, devoid enough of cars that we don't have to follow the curve around to the light to cross over. And down the wide, shallow steps.

When Paris ceases to be a silhouette or a mirage and instead becomes a place where people simply go about their days, making their lives; where the Métro herkily jerks along; where some portion of the city always seems to be on strike, and it's not uncommon to get a faint whiff of tear gas when Vélib'ing through Place de la République; where it's impossible to buy Advil in packs of more than ten for less than seven euros, buy nail polish for less than fifteen euros, get a package delivered, or even just find affordable quality sushi; it can be, if not shocking, then surprising, to encounter the Paris of the films. Of the fantasy.

But it does exist. And it's waiting for us now.

The first time Nina and I met for a drink four years ago we went to an outdoor bar along the river, a short distance from Notre-Dame, just off the wide walking path thronged with tourists. It had been her choice, and I'd assumed it was a measure of how little she really knew Paris. It felt to me like asking someone to dinner in Times Square. But actually, it turned out that I was the one who didn't understand. The carafes of rosé were regularly priced and there were plenty of Parisians there, perhaps more Parisians than not. It was the first time it occurred to me Paris is not demarcated by tourists the way New York is, with prices doubling in concert with people's increasing lack of awareness of their space. Parisians use Paris the way serious hunters I knew in Wyoming used the entire carcass of the beast they'd just struck down; they do not leave the good parts for scavengers.

Tonight, the Seine is seemingly entirely French. Blankets spread out, prime spots under trees already secured. Everywhere cigarette smoke and open bottles of wine.

Ellie and Aarti are already here. They've marked out a spot across the pathway that separates us from the river, under a tree whose roots are upending the cobblestone. We are only a few feet from the stone wall that rises high above us to the street. The wall is where men come to pee when the lineup for the porta-potty is too long, and sometimes even when it's not. Ellie is frustrated there is no space closer to the river, but it seems everyone left in Paris has come down here tonight.

I'm wearing a red cotton tank dress I bought a few days earlier at Monoprix for twelve euros. Few of the outfits I hauled across the ocean, and sweatily lugged up the stairs, have left the apartment. Even the rose gold Birks I almost never take off at home have remained in my flat. It only took one long walk to dinner in the 9th on my third night before I scurried to buy a pair of the omnipresent white tennis shoes. How had I not understood their attractiveness before? Or is it just the comfort of doing what everyone else is doing. I may not speak the actual language, but I can participate thusly. These shoes are what I have on now, with thin white socks underneath also purchased at Monoprix. None of the selves I'd spent more than a year envisioning had yet to find a place here. Currently Paris is requiring me to be only one person, and that person is currently wearing tight-fitting cheap cotton.

Sandra arrives with Marcel, red scarf tied around his neck, and a wicker picnic basket that holds a blanket, the foodstuff, utensils, and napkins. Also, a jar of kimchi. We shift into motion as if someone has flipped a switch. Spreading the blanket out, pinning the edges down with bags, or in my case, with my shoes, which I have removed. Spreading out all our wares and passing around glasses. The conversation ongoing—continued from yesterday, from last weekend—seems like the Paris light: immersive and glowing and disconnected from sharp details that pin it down. More a feeling than a narrative.

The late afternoon begins its gentle slide into evening. The crippled towers of Notre-Dame, visible in the distance, begin to glow slightly as the sky slowly shifts to a darker blue. We are halfway through the second bottle of rosé when a band sets up not far away from us. In summers past, I have often seen swing dancing accompanied by live music, farther down the Seine. But this band is not that. Something that is immediately clear when they begin playing. After cringing through a warm-up that has us questioning whether we need to pack up entirely and move to a different location, they move into nineties indie rock, drowning out our conversation. Oh god, our looks say to each other, why do dudes need to ruin everything (not entirely fair, since one of the singers appears to be a young woman). The only thing that keeps us here is the inability to summon the energy to not be here. Instead of packing up the sliced saucisson, it's easier just to eat it. A friend of Sandra's, a woman about our age wearing a T-shirt and jeans and the same white runners I have on, wanders by and joins us. I don't catch her name in introductions, but she gestures back in the direction she came to suggest there is another group if we want to join them. But instead another bottle gets opened and Sandra, who is more irritated by the situation than any of us, throws her hands down on her lap in exasperation. Marcel does not like loud noises.

And the band is loud. I suppose it's not possible to play a Soundgarden song quietly, which is what they are doing. The absurdity of it all begins to work its charm; perhaps it's just the novelty of live music, or maybe it's just that the musicians are clearly enjoying themselves. Soon a group gathers round. After the janky warm-up, it only takes a few songs before one person begins to move differently, and like a spark on dry tinder the small crowd bursts forth together; the clapping turns to dancing, and as the sky moves from sapphire into gold, turning the waters into thin strokes of fire, we find ourselves adjacent to a full-blown dance party that is soon blocking the wide pathway. Actually, I can't tell if the crowd is blocking the path or if, like a strangely angled branch in a stream, the dancers are just collecting passersby. Certainly, no one seems like they want to move on. The energy is contagious. Small children climb out of passing strollers, cyclists shrug off their irritation at having their path blocked and dismount, joining the swaying crowd with one hand on their handlebars. Joggers stop and bounce in place.

As though I'm a cartoon character floating away on an enticing scent, I rise and walk across the cobblestones in my cheap red dress and socks. Ellie comes with me, and together we join the circle and slide into the music.

It feels like my first drink of water after a long trek across the desert. Like plunging into a cool lake after a day of sweat and grime. I have missed touch, yes, and I have missed conversation, and I have missed being with my friends. But the energy of so many people moving together is something I didn't know I wanted. It's intoxicating. More than that. It's ecstatic. In the original sense of the word, which is derived from the Greek verb *existanai*, meaning "entrancement, astonishment, insanity; any displacement or removal from the proper place." Proper or otherwise, I have been removed. And right now, I'm in the only place I want to be. I feel as though I am in a state of rapture. I am fully and completely in my own body in a way I have not been in such a long time, I wonder right now if there was ever really a time that I was.

Almost immediately, I lose Ellie in the crowd but it doesn't matter. No one is leaving without telling me. We are all women accustomed to moving about the world on our own, and as such keep strong trained eyes on one another even from great distances. From across oceans. But also, practically, I know my way home. I always know my way home from wherever I am, and at the moment I'm approximately an eighteen-minute walk from my bed.

Soon even these minor thoughts are pushed out of my head by the beat and the bodies. Nirvana. 4 Non Blondes. I wonder if the people playing these songs were even alive when they were played on the radio or if they are simply trying to connect themselves to a time where the norm was to be in only one place at one time.

And then somehow amidst the crowd there is just one body.

I'm dancing with a tall, muscular man. He's wearing a red tank top that matches my dress and shows off his bulging arms. He's in khaki shorts and silver high-top runners. I move toward him and then spin away, twirling around the other dancers with the music, but each time I seem to find myself back in his sphere. Soon he takes my hand and tries to slip into a proper dance with me. I laugh and shake my head. I can't dance. I think of the ranch in Wyoming where I spent the month of August the year I turned forty. The girls who worked there were taught square dancing from a young age and I would watch them fly across the floor, spinning and kicking, always knowing what their partner would do and where they would be. I'm envious of the skill. I've never learned any kind of dance, and even if I had, I question whether it would have made much difference. I only ever seem to be coordinated on a bike, or in the water; the rest of the time I'm clumsy and awkward, barely managing to walk a straight line on the sidewalk.

But he persists and I slide my phone under my left bra strap, so I have both hands free, shrug off my ingrained concerns, and lean into his body, and into the music, and somewhat miraculously we manage to move into a coordinated rhythm. Or at least that's what it feels like. His hands move to my back, pressing and guiding me, and then they eventually (or immediately . . . I have become entirely disconnected from the clock) slide lower, landing firmly on either hip. I turn my head up and, as if guided by some force disconnected from my brain, my own hands move under his shirt, and I feel the sweaty muscles undulating to the music. And then eventually, or immediately, we are kissing. Somewhere, very far back in my brain, moving further even as it tries to make itself heard, a small, deeply unconvincing voice wants me to know that kissing strangers in a pandemic that is fast moving into a worrisome second wave is not responsible behavior. But I am hurtling away from that voice, or it from me, too quickly for it to make any impact. I have been careful for a year. What I *am* aware of are his hands on my body, slipping further down, and then the small voice disappears entirely. Along with it, as though sucked into a black hole, disappears any awareness of myself from the outside. Gone are all the reflections of myself I have depended on for the last year, what feels like an eternity. Gone is the understanding of myself from the me I see looking back. Gone is the me who existed to so many loved ones only from the neck up, in a square box staring back at me from a screen. I am fully inside myself and only looking out. I don't care how I appear, only how I feel, and I feel fucking fantastic right now.

Eventually my dance partner and I manage some broken conversation through the music and the kissing and the touching and the groping. He is from Senegal. He likes dancing. I'm from New York. I'm in Paris *en vacances pour un mois.*

This is the sum total of information we exchange in our time together. I guess his age at around thirty, give or take. We return to our bodies.

Sometime after midnight the band stops playing, and the crowd begins to disperse. From the corner of my eye, I'm vaguely aware of my group packing up our things. There is a sliver of moon high over the now dark water. The black silhouette of Notre-Dame is barely visible against the sky.

My dance partner conveys to me he might be going dancing at another club in the 13th. I'm not going with him. Even through the fog of rosé and the high of our dancing, I shirk from the idea of having to find a new way home, *especially* through the fog of rosé. This has been delightful, I'm happy to go home. We kiss goodbye. And then again. And again. His hands sliding from my neck, down to my thighs, and then back up again. I slide mine into his hair, pulling him closer, until even after midnight on the Seine we are verging on the obscene. I pull out my phone from where it is still wedged in my bra strap, the screen dripping with my own sweat.

"WhatsApp?" I say to him.

He looks skeptical, but when I hand him the phone, he enters his number.

"*Merci.*" I kiss him. "I will message," I say.

He nods. I can tell he's not convinced. I'm not convinced either, but it feels wonderful to have options.

"His hands were all over you!" Sandra's friend tells me when I finally return to our blanket and push my swollen feet, socks filthy-black on the bottom now, into my waiting tennis shoes.

Her tone cuts through the fog of ecstasy I am in, suggesting I should . . . be scandalized? Feel shame? At the very least I should be embarrassed. I recognize it immediately as my own voice coming to greet me from other times and places when I'd admonished friends for doing things that deep down I wished I was doing. Or even just wished I was capable of doing. I don't know Sandra's friend at all, but

I understand what she really means is: I'm scared to do the thing you just did, and you doing it made me have to think about that.

"That's exactly where I wanted them to be," I say with a smile.

This, I think, is what maturity actually means most of the time. It has little to do with growing away from the things that bring us pleasure or joy or just silly fun. It most often just means kindness. Knowing how to give it, to ourselves and others, and also receive it. In this instance, this is not a challenge since I'm so high on the sensation of my entire body being alive I cannot feel anything but good. Beyond good, I feel great. I'm surprised by how powerful I feel. I got what I wanted, or allowed what I wanted to get me.

Nina and I walk home, still swaying to the music. When she drops me off, I tell her to text me as soon as she's in. We've done this so many times together. Upstairs I lie on the floor. Whatever remained of my rational brain a short while ago, the one that thought the dancing and kissing and touching were enough, has gone as silent as the cautionary voice in my head that made its feeble stand earlier. I don't regret not going dancing somewhere in the 13th, but I'm not done with the night. I swipe through my Fruitz messages to see if there's potential for some fun chat. There are a slew of messages waiting for me, but immediately I realize I want more. I want the real thing. I decide I should message my dance partner. Even through the high of the evening this feels a bit insane. Does one message a stranger from the dance floor? Isn't it enough to know I *could* message him? I consider this for a few minutes. It is not. We've all been living in a place of balancing risk against caution for what feels like a long time, and very little feels like enough right now. I open WhatsApp and type:

"Come over?"

The worst that can happen is he says no, I think as I hit send.

The response is immediate.

"Où es-tu?"

I send the address before my brain has a chance to reemerge. I know what I want.

"En route. Dix minutes."

"Bien," I type. The sensation of being wanted immediately. I get up to brush my teeth. My stomach churning through the wine at the imminent reality. My phone pings again, and a bolt of worry that he's changed his mind shoots through me—the disappointment is telling. I'm not drunk or playing; I really *do* want this. But it's not him, it's just Nina telling me she's home. I send back three thumbs-up emojis. I hesitate. Should I tell her? I should. But I don't.

When I'm done brushing my teeth, I double-check that the box of condoms I brought with me is in the bedside table. Then I return to the living room and lean out the window. The streets are quiet, it's close to 2:00 a.m. now. The night air is cool, and the city glows against the low clouds above. I turn to the left and see his figure coming down the street. I watch for a minute, alert with the power that I have summoned this. I have been summoning this for months and now it's here. I knew what I wanted and I got it. I don't wait for him to get to the door, or even message. We've already done the dance. Literally. I've invited him here for one reason. I take the keys, shut the door firmly behind me, and hurry down the stairs, the marble cool against my bare feet, and am at the door when he arrives. This is a New York habit, established from years of living in brownstones with no buzzers. The fact I could have just given him the front door code and simply waited at the door, eliminating any need for stilted small talk, does not register as an option, even though Aarti once told me she gives her door code to every delivery man. Between the restaurants that share access to the lobby, all the occupants of the building, and all the people they invite in, who knows how many people have this code.

In the small time we've been apart I've already forgotten how tall he is. How broad. The strong smell of too much cologne wafts off him. He follows me up the flights of stairs, not touching me. "One more *étage*," I say, thinking the stairs suddenly seem endless. I wonder how this will go. Will it be awkward? No one has seen me naked for a long time. But when I close the door to the apartment, I simply turn to him, and smiling at one another, we immediately pick up where we left off. This time there is no sense of propriety slowing down the removal of my clothes. Which are immediately removed. By him.

As my dress comes off, and then my bra, I consider what my nude, forty-six-year-old body might look like to outside eyes. It does not look like the bodies we are told *should* be naked. It is not a defying *can you believe it* body. It has not fared as well as my face. It has shouldered the highs and the plunges of life, of grief, and loss, and confusion, and self-deception, and the reliable joys of food, and the months where not exercising was definitely the healthier option. It is the body of a person who can no longer skate by on no health insurance. Who must follow up on every scan. Who cannot leave home even for one night without tweezers. Who can barely conceive of wearing heels because of the pain they cause my feet.

Should I be concerned? Get under the covers first? Try to angle myself so that the fact one breast currently points in the wrong direction thanks to last year's biopsy is less noticeable? So that the dimples down the backs of my thighs can only be felt instead of seen?

It doesn't matter.

None of these questions need answering. The concerns disappear more quickly than they arrive. Now that I'm here, in my body and out of my head, I find I don't care. I can't even make myself care. I'm being carried away by all the things that get lost in a two-dimensional world where our eyes are the only way to interact with others, where all our other senses are replaced with an immediate search for "flaws."

What gets lost in that world: The headiness of another body, the smells, the awkwardness, the vulnerability. Small puffs of air on bare skin. The presence of another person, taking up space, shifting every-thing in the room so that it takes on a different significance: the lumpy, detestable couch now a helpful place to balance a knee on. The doorframe a solid scaffolding to remain upright. And then, the glori-ous sensation of just being naked. Skin. So much skin. Hands where there haven't been hands in . . . who knows how long. And more skin. More than anything I have missed the contact of skin.

I look up to see him staring at me and I catch that look on his face, the look we are relentlessly told is reserved only for the rarified who have followed the proper regime. Applied the toners and moisturizers and serums in the *correct* order. Lifted the right amount of weights. Done cardio for the correct amount of time. Excluded the right amount of sugar or fats or meats. Followed each set of new rules as they appear. Restricted themselves. Contorted themselves. Done the work. Remained young. It is the look of a man gazing upon a naked female body they have been invited to partake in. A mix of lust, ex-citement, gratitude, and relief.

He steps back for a moment, dropping my bra onto the couch and removing his shirt. He takes another long look at me. Ah the enjoyment of being enjoyed. "Amazing," he says with a grin before coming closer. And I think, Yes. *Yes.* You *are* fortunate my clothes are off. It *is* amazing.

Is there a name for the Male Gaze being subverted by actual male gazes?

No matter whose individual direct gaze we find ourselves under—how that individual might identify, how you might—we are all existing under the Male Gaze. Even when we work to live outside of it. Even to define your life as being outside of it is, itself, a recognition of what and who is inside. Who is offered the sanctuary. This Male Gaze has so many names. Patriarchy. Women's clothing sizes. Beauty products. Pay rates. Health care. It's endless. To step outside of it even for a moment is to risk casting yourself into a void. Because what else is out there? It's nearly impossible to know. And then perhaps you do anyway. Because you have to. Or maybe, as in my case, just because I can. And very briefly you find, for instance, yourself in the literal gaze of an extremely attractive young man no one has ever suggested you'd be in the gaze of again. And you are reminded, even just briefly, that it's all a lie. For them as much as for you.

It's in the face of this expression that I remember something I've always known. Not learned. Known. Far from cataloging the state of your breasts, or your hips, or your tummy, men are mostly just thrilled you've taken off your clothes at all. Women's bodies are beautiful. Truly. All of them. The amount of energy that has gone into convincing us otherwise is extraordinary and telling. The fact I am currently being reminded of this by a thirty-year-old man with bulging arms and a washboard stomach—that I *need* to be reminded of this by a man—feels like a somewhat problematic catch-22 that I imagine has been explored in a number of highly respected feminist books I have not read. Nor do I particularly care about them in this moment. All I want is more skin. More and more and more. More skin. More hands. More everything. And for the next five hours that is exactly what I get. Again and again and again.

NINE

The Assumption

My dance partner showers and leaves as the sun is coming up. A pleasant goodbye. A perhaps we will see each other again, but also the implicit understanding that this was lovely and enough. I feel as though I'm inside life again. No longer thinking about how to get there and wondering if I ever will. I fall asleep, satisfied.

I wake up hours later, sore from my night of dancing. From being twisted and contorted to accommodate another person's body. I feel used up in exactly the right way. Destroyed in the way Hemingway meant it, "the good destruction . . . the way we're made to be destroyed." Aware of the totality of my physical presence. I immediately lose count of the bells, but it must be close to noon. It's Sunday. The middle of August. Very little will be open today. The city has closed up shop for the remainder of the month.

The day is far too beautiful to stay inside, no matter how much my body is currently protesting the excess of alcohol and lack of sleep, and when I finally leave the apartment I aim for the Jardin des Plantes, just across the river; Jardin du Luxembourg seems like too much effort. No biking for me today. I have no plans other than simply to sit. To be.

Which is what I do. It's only when the light becomes so beautiful and I feel compelled to capture it in some way that I pull out my phone and see that Silhouette—a man I matched with early on, whose profile photo is merely a silhouette—has messaged me. He's back from holiday and would like to meet me in the 6th for a drink, and some conversation, during which we will decide whether to make plans to meet again for other exchanges presumably involving less talking and more nudity. It's all very civilized. It's the sort of conversation a person who enjoys Catherine Deneuve films imagines grownups having in Paris.

My indecision about whether to go is partly due to how content I'm feeling right now; the park is so beautiful and the light so nice. And partly to do with the fact that last night's shift from fantasy to very satisfying reality has left me feeling confident in an entirely new way. Enjoyment, the real-life kind involving skin on skin on skin, is mine for the taking. I simply have to say yes. If I don't say yes today, I can simply say it tomorrow.

But the messages sit there. I like the thought that has been put into them. Not here's what I'd like to do in theory, but specific plans. We will go here, then, if we desire, we will go there.

And so eventually I get up and make my slow way across quiet Paris.

.   .   .   .

Rue des Écoles is a street I know well. Over the years, I've biked across it in the early hours to get to the Lux for a morning run. But now, on foot, the buildings without the people seem removed from their familiar geography in my brain. Paris is distorted in its emptiness. I feel as though I have slipped out of the Paris I know, into some other shadow Paris.

I can hear the voices before I see them. At first it sounds like singing coming from a far-off radio on another street out an open window. Someone listening to the broadcast of a church service. And then it fades away. But only briefly. The voices return. Louder now, soaring up against the buildings. The sound against the stone makes the walls seem taller than they are. Rue des Écoles runs directly east-west and is one of the streets on this side of the river that give Paris the semblance of a grid. The Left Bank was less carved out by Haussmann than the Right; I'm technically in the Latin Quarter right now, though here on Écoles, skirting the heart of it, where the side streets and lanes can get truly twisty.

Above, the sky is a blue dome. It's warm but not punishing. I'm wearing cropped white jeans and a white linen tank top and white tennis shoes. One of the apps tells me which of my photos is the most popular, and apparently, it's the one of me in this tank, sitting down, my tummy bulging slightly above the waistband of these jeans. Its popularity is another reminder that the way sex is sold to women is not always how men receive it. I catch a reflection of myself in a store window and snap a photo. Yes, this is fine. I would be happy to see this arrive if I were waiting on the other end. After we first matched, Silhouette told me he was happy to send me photos of himself, but I rather liked the mystery of not knowing. A rarity these days. Then I became so distracted by all the other messages I simply forgot to follow up. Who knows what's waiting for me.

The singing is not from a radio. That is clear. Perhaps there is an actual church service nearby, it is Sunday, after all. I pass Rue Saint-Jacques, where I usually make a left on my bike. The long, unbroken wall of the Sorbonne stands like a parapet against the empty street. We're always told, likely apocryphally, that the Inuit have many words for snow but how many words can I come up with for empty, an experience equally as fascinating and enjoyable to my mind in a world this connected.

It's here I meet the singers.

They are a part of a long procession that stretches to my right down Rue Saint-Jacques toward Notre-Dame, and then ahead on Rue des Écoles. Parisians. Hundreds, perhaps. Dressed in their Sunday clothes, some casual, some adhering to the old Catholicism of my grandmother who could not conceive of entering a church with her head uncovered. Hymnbooks in hand, they are walking together solemnly, and joyfully it seems, their voices rising up and falling like a wave. I walk with them, allowing the music to wash over and carry me. Grateful for the unexpected beauty of the moment. The streets are otherwise vacant. There are no observers to raise their cameras and peel its vitality away to relay it to other eyes. This isn't a performance, it's a celebration.

It must be a religious holiday, but I can't think of which one. My mother referred to our sort of Catholicism as the cafeteria kind: take what you like and leave the rest. I bolted the church at the age of thir-teen, when I switched myself from Catholic school to public high school after eighth grade. No thank you. Outside of Easter and Christmas and a vague awareness of Ash Wednesday, all the many holidays of the church are beyond me.

I pull out my phone from my back pocket to google the signifi-cance of today's date, August 15. But before I can I'm distracted by a *New York Times* alert waiting for me on my screen. Kabul has fallen. The Taliban are retaking the city.

These strange wrinkles in time.

I rarely talk, or even think too hard, about what it was actually like to be in New York on September 11. That narrative was yanked away from everyone who experienced it directly and handed to the world as a universal experience, and eventually a bludgeon. A shared tragedy that doesn't allow for the individual somehow. In that regard, at least, a bit like these last eighteen months.

Next month will mark twenty years since September 11, and only now, with this news, does the actual feeling of that day come rushing back in. The smells, the disbelief, the dread. As though we were just there. That day and this day strange bookends to a story about how much, and how little, can change at the same time.

I scan the *New York Times* report. My international data plan in-sists on loading everything slowly, presumably to drive me to pay for faster access. I'm only able to catch glimpses of what's happening in Kabul as it flickers on and off the screen. The mad dash. The stam-peding of airport runways. The young men clinging to the wheels of planes as they take off. The great desperation to leave.

I think of the women. An entire generation of women raised to believe their lives would look different from their mothers' and grand-mothers' and so on and so on. Where are they running to right now? I think.

I look down at my own feet. My white Parisian tennis shoes are now appropriately scuffed up. I think of the steps I am taking right now versus the steps those women are also taking right now. Walking together somehow, even as we are separated by so much.

I have unwittingly picked up my pace and am nearing the head of the procession. I can see some sort of statue being held aloft down the line. I return to my phone to finish my original search. What church holiday is August 15? The music around me soars and then quiets. I scan the faces of the procession, worried it has ended. But it hasn't. They are simply starting a new song. Finally, a result on my phone. It's the Day of Assumption. It's the day the church celebrates Mary being lifted, body and soul, into heaven without having to experience the degradation of death. Having spent her life never having had to experience the degradation of sex or, presumably, orgasm. No having the watercress grazed for Mother Mary.

Before leaving the flat, I'd seen a tweet by the Pope noting that "Mary's secret is humility." It was, he wrote, "her humility that attracted God's gaze to her." I'd briefly wondered what had prompted the observation. Now I understood the significance.

Humility: "having a lowly opinion of oneself; meekness, lowliness, humbleness." Which no doubt, has been interpreted in a myriad of ways, but to me mostly sounds like just another way to say be quiet. Stop talking. Take up less space. It's just a hop, skip, and syllable away from humiliation. Which somehow makes me think of all the women who have told me they are too humiliated to be seen eating alone.

I think of all the women, however many miles and time zones away, barely mentioned in the news report on my phone, who have spent the last twenty years contemplating the possibility of a life that involved less humility and more agency. Alone time. How this day will likely mark the last day of so much for them; the abrupt end of whatever narrative they've been formulating for themselves these last twenty years.

And here I am, the same twenty years later, my steps leading in another direction entirely. I am on the far, far periphery of their story. Barely visible. Inconsequential in this moment. Even if they remain in my meditations.

I keep walking.

The figure I spotted earlier being held aloft is, of course, Mary. Virginal. Glorious. Standing on her throne. Behind her walk a handful of priests in their white and black robes. Bareheaded. And behind them, hidden by the procession until now, are fifty or so nuns. Two by two, in two straight lines. Their habits black, their long robes white; rosaries in hand, skirts swinging as they march. They are beautiful and powerful. They are poetry.

The singing begins again. I keep pace with the nuns.

I know I am supposed to feel shame. Shame that I am here. Enjoying myself. While elsewhere right now so many others are not. Elsewhere in the world, right this second, the only steps women are able to take are on the run, back inside. And here, to my right, the swinging clothes of the marching nuns, another sort of cloistering. What right do I have to enjoy myself in this moment? I automatically ask myself. And then, immediately: What right do I have not to? What right do I have not to take the joy that is available to me?

The voices of the procession rise again. They feel like a balm, but also a prayer. At Boulevard Saint-Michel the procession turns right. I stop at the corner, the sky still a blue dome above, and watch them ripple down to the bridge, the singing slowly fading away. And then I turn away and I keep going.

I know within seconds of meeting Silhouette that I am not interested. The most interesting things about him are all the things I have layered on to the blank slate of his profile; and in the end they are a reflection of me, things I think I want and am still projecting on to others.

I wonder later if the look on my face when we first meet makes this clear. No, it must say. I'm aware that I do not wonder whether he is thinking the same; that perhaps I was not as I had visually presented myself. Not what he'd been hoping for.

He leads me through some streets that I don't pay attention to, to a café he tells me is somewhat famous. After we sit, a young couple who appears to have stepped out of a nineties perfume ad—they are both so beautiful—sit opposite. They are directly in my line of view and I have trouble diverting my gaze. What sort of lives come attached to that sort of beauty? Beauty as the inciting incident, which for women in myths, never ends well.

We navigate around conversation as though we are in a museum remarking on the intellectual attributes of the paintings. The terrible news out of Afghanistan. The politics of Paris's mayor. Check. Check. He is amused that I come here in August. "There are no Parisians!"

Something about the way he makes reference to my life in New York being big, "There must be a lot of people there happy for you to return," makes me think he thinks I am married. There are, in fact, a lot of people who will be happy for me to return, but I don't provide any clarity. He references his children. He says they're currently away in the South. I don't ask any questions. What do I need to know, really. He says when he returns to Paris the next weekend he will make hotel reservations somewhere. Okay, I say noncommittally. Am I required to do a face-to-face breakup with a person I have just met, whose name I don't know? I don't think so. I'm not obligated to do much of anything right now, something I am electrically aware of today. I unmatch him on my way to meet Ellie for dinner. There's more enjoyment to be had elsewhere.

Grazing the Watercress

The switch has been flipped. As though I am constructed of a million tiny bulbs and someone, me, cried, *Que la lumière soit!* It is no longer a matter of my carefully scrolling through the apps; now I simply go with my gut at first sight. If they look handsome. If they look interesting. If I like the cut of their shirt. If words happen to jump out that appeal—the fewer the better; long bios are not enjoyable—I say yes. Age becomes a useless metric. I move "I'm mostly here to enjoy myself" into my bio. Lead with your needs. As much as I enjoy hearing some descriptions of how all these men— and there are so many—want to help me enjoy myself, I no longer need it. I know what I want: more of the same.

On the Tuesday after dancing by the Seine I arrive home on the early side. There are no friend plans tonight; the evening stretches before me like an arid desert. This will not do. My skin, far from being satiated, is hungrier than ever. Several of the chat threads on my app are now over a week old, ancient in chat time. These men have begun to feel familiar. I message Blindfold, one of the men whom I'd first required to walk me through all the ways he planned to make sure I enjoyed myself. Would he come over?

Twenty minutes later he tells me he will be there in thirty minutes.

I don't lie naked in bed waiting for him. My current sense of adventure does not yet (and may never) extend to leaving the door unlocked or handing out door codes. Nor does he arrive with a blind-fold. It will have to be a quick meeting, he tells me, apologetically. He wanted to see me, he says, but this would be short and direct. He has family members who have arrived unexpectedly. He can't stay long. I worry he will go into more detail about family stress, that despite my not asking questions, this was going to turn into a therapy session. But he says no more. He is just being polite, I realize. He doesn't want the quickness of this visit to reflect badly on either of us. He looks like his photo, tall and lanky with a dark head of hair. Handsome in a late-nineties British indie band sort of way. And clean. Very French. I guess his age to be close to mine, but between the slimness and the slightly long hair, it's hard to tell.

He asks where the kitchen is, washes his hands, and gets a glass of water. My enjoyment is the priority, not his.

Great.

And so strange.

I am in a flimsy silk caftan and nothing else. He is in black jeans and a black T-shirt. His black boots sit by the door.

"Is this your first time doing this sort of thing?" he asks. By "this sort of thing," I assume he means summoning a stranger to my home for the very specific, one-sided experience of my pleasure, which does not involve actual sex. I can't decide if I felt flattered by the question or a little disappointed at the possibility I have been so easily read. Did I not appear to be a person who did this sort of thing? Who comfortably commanded men to my door when desire struck? Was I evincing naivete, or an American tourist on the prowl?

The truth, of course, is that I am all these things. And happy to be so. But I wasn't sure I liked to be so obvious about it. Was it possible to be mysterious and also declare exactly what you wanted?

I shrugged. "Perhaps?"

He smiles. "Why don't you take your dress off?"

I do.

So strange to have so much skin exposed, not to other skin but to the rough fabric of denim and cotton. A habitual sense of vulnerability mixes with electric currents of power that come with calling all the shots about your own body.

Hunger satiated. Twice.

TEN

A Moveable Feast

Waiting for me in Paris is Miss Fisher. Like a pleasant smell, or a dish, I forget she is here until I arrive. And then she calls to me.

I found her on Netflix during my first August visit here, in 2016, when the city felt empty not just of Parisians but of friendship and ties. The intensity of that loneliness was all-encompassing. I had almost no knowledge of Paris. Away from wireless internet, my international phone plan at the time allowed for only a few minutes of good connection a day before my monthly bill threatened to quadruple. My French was truly abysmal. But more than actual language, I did not understand the rhythms of the city at all. I would find myself leaving the apartment at what felt like a late hour, 3:00 p.m., after finishing my work, with the overwhelming sense that I'd missed the day. But Paris does not really come alive until after lunch, and I was relieved to discover I could live a whole entire other day between

3:00 and 10:00. Days of scorching solitude. The summer sun sets later in Paris. While it was shining, my aloneness wasn't so apparent to me, but in the evening, when I would wander down Boulevard Henri IV, and along the Seine, it felt like a presence emanating from me in waves. Language bounced off me. Other people's conversation flowed around me but could not carry me away. Even as I marveled at my location, the glow of Notre-Dame against the sky visible long before I could see it and the spotlight of the Eiffel Tower swinging like a pendulum across the sky, I felt seared by solitude. A separate being entirely from the groups at cafés. The groups on blankets along the river. Families together in parks, even the ones who were clearly tourists.

That intensity leapt off and infused everything I encountered. The city vibrated with remote strangeness. That degree of newness and intensity slows time. It feels similar to the experience of trying to walk through deep water. There were days I didn't think I could bear it. Like the pressure of it would succeed in pulverizing me.

It was in this cone of social silence that I found Miss Fisher.

Miss Fisher's Murder Mysteries is an Australian show based on a series of lighthearted mystery novels written by a woman named Kerry Greenwood. Miss Fisher is a wealthy flapper (raised poor, her family came into money sometime after her poverty-stricken childhood, though the show never makes clear exactly how) who has returned to post–World War I Melbourne and designated herself a lady detective. In the novels she is in her early twenties. A vision of the new woman. Beautiful, fashionable, fun. Zelda Fitzgerald without the husband or the mental illness. There are twenty-three Miss Fisher novels, but despite repeated best efforts I've never finished reading a single one. It's the rare case of the television show elevating its source material into something deeper and more satisfying.

I credit this to the fact the people in charge of the show (I'm assuming women) decided that instead of staying true to the book and casting a twenty-something actress to play the role of the protagonist Phryne Fisher, they would instead cast the then forty-year-old actress Essie Davis. Subsequently, our television Phryne is no ingénue. She has been a nurse on the front lines, a muse for Parisian surrealists (one of the first episodes involves a painting of her reclined naked, pubic hair on display, which has been stolen from her home, where it prominently hangs), and now a fearless figure who commands a household, is best friends with a lesbian surgeon (who sports perfectly tailored tweed suits), and whose assistant, Dot, is tasked early on with returning Phryne's diaphragm to its container. Phryne has a smoldering unrequited love affair with Detective Inspector Jack Robinson, while also engaging in sexual trysts with a new man each week, often remorselessly turning them in to the police after she discovers they are the guilty party.

Amazingly, it took me some time to realize the reason I loved Phryne, and continually returned to her, was not just the exquisite clothes, or the perfect Louise Brooks hair, or the fact that no matter how many times I watched an episode I could never remember the plot and so it always somehow seemed new. It was because she was a *grown-up*. She was not getting married. She was not having children ("I don't understand the appeal," she likes to say). Her power was not in her potential to be matched up. Her power was her. Full stop. It was so satisfying.

I think often about how the best stories we have about women outside of marriage and motherhood are almost always about women detectives. Their lives alone, literally and figuratively, are not enough to support what we understand as narrative, and so the most basic, most recognizable narrative is attached to them: whodunnit. In this extremely formalized structure, they are allowed to float along, being messy, or complicated, or elderly, or fashionable. We understand their purpose. Phryne's real purpose, of course, is to live well, and love well, and do exactly what she pleases. What she brings to me, and what she brought to me that first summer of warping loneliness, was the comfort that all narratives bring: recognition and companionship.

I still return to Miss Fisher when I'm here, even though Paris no longer vibrates the way it once did. Every year it becomes more familiar. I sometimes find myself missing the intensity of that solitude even as I relish the power of my knowledge and friendships.

Which is not to say I *know* Paris. I don't. How could I when I am still lurching through the language like a drunk toddler? But it is no longer a stranger.

I do wonder if it's even possible to truly know Paris. Are there old-school taxi drivers out there who made their living before GPS and whose brains are self-contained maps of every side street and courtyard? Paris, to me, often feels like a series of islands, an archipelago of recognizable spots I come upon without ever being entirely sure how I arrived. The strange result is that in one of the most touristed cities on earth I'm sometimes left with the sense that I alone have discovered a certain corner, a small square, a curved side street. Only to find out, after some very brief googling, that in fact, my hidden corner was at one time the road to Rome.

Maybe Paris feels so unknowable because it does not ask one to have a destination at all times. It's fine just to be. To wander. The irony of knowing Paris better is I feel less compelled to see it. Routines have been established, and as my social circles grow larger and richer, the actual circles I travel in grow smaller. Where I used to venture out, trying to make the city more familiar with my feet, I can now go weeks without leaving the equivalent of a ten-block radius.

It's this feeling of having come but not seen that pushes me out the door one afternoon. After two weeks in Paris spent relishing all my friendships, much of the city still feels remote. So, I take to the streets. Ellie is a walker like me and is officially on holiday this week. I tell her I'm going to walk over to Montparnasse and visit my favorite apartment building in Paris, and she says she'll meet me there.

I came across this particular apartment building one afternoon a few years ago after trying to locate a children's store I remembered being charmingly novel so I could purchase a gift for one of my many godchildren. I'd made a wrong turn and ended up on a quiet side street that faced onto Cimetière du Montparnasse. What immediately caught my well-trained real estate eye were the double-height windows. So much of Paris is uniform Haussmann that deviations stand out. The windows on this building were probably twenty-five feet high and nearly as wide. Four floors of them. The roof had slanted skylights. It exuded Art Deco. I was mesmerized.

You can't visit apartments online in Paris the way you can in New York (*privé!*)—I have the floor plans of nearly every doorman building on Central Park West, West End Avenue, and a number of East Side Rosario Candelas committed to memory. If I wanted to fantasize about life in this particular apartment, I had to come to Montparnasse in person, so I could take it in from a different angle, perhaps from across the street where I could get a better view of the upper floors, or maybe get a glimpse inside depending on the time of day, and state of the curtains. It was like visiting a person, except I was really visiting a different, imagined version of my life. I'd spent not a little time on Airbnb trying to discover if anyone in the building ever rented their homes out, but so far, no luck.

I don't recall which visit it was that I noticed the plaque.

Simone de Beauvoir

1908–1986

Auteur du Deuxième Sexe

Écrivain, Philosophe

Vécut dans Cette Maison

De 1955 à 1986

I must confess, this was only of minimal interest to me. I know who Simone de Beauvoir is, of course, and possess some basic knowledge of her feminist writings. In recent years her books have been reissued, and while they had not reached a Didion-level frenzy, the hot pink cover of *The Woman Destroyed* (which I have not read) with its green lips and a dangling cigarette had been regularly making its way across my Instagram feed as some sort of feminist stigmata to demonstrate one had done the work, or was doing the work, or at least understood the assignment.

Nor can I claim more than the basic knowledge of *The Second Sex*, though when I do pick it up, I'm sometimes struck by the fact I seem to be living some version of it. Beauvoir writes of "the metaphysical risk of a freedom that must invent its goals without help," which is a risk I feel like I've been encountering regularly for some time now, but have never shied from. Reading Beauvoir sometimes felt like seeing the taped outline of my body at a crime scene. Yes, I could see myself, but only approximately. I preferred action, not theory.

So perhaps it's not surprising that the Simone de Beauvoir book I hold close is *America Day by Day*. Her travelogue of visiting the United States in 1947. In the prologue she writes:

I spent four months in America—very little time. Furthermore, I traveled for pleasure and wherever I happened to be invited. . . . In place of serious study, which would be presumptuous for me to attempt, I can offer a faithful account [of my travels]. Because concrete experience involves both subject and object, I have not tried to eliminate myself from this narrative: it is truthful only because it includes the unique personal circumstances in which each discovery was made.

Her travel journals were initially published in France in 1948 (two years before *The Second Sex*), and in America in 1952 (five years before *On the Road*). Then they disappeared for about four decades. (This disappearing act calls to mind *West with the Night*, Beryl Markham's extraordinary memoir of her childhood in Africa along with being the first person to fly across the Atlantic, east to west. *West with the Night* published in 1942, and then vanished for about five decades until it was revived by a small publishing press with a quote from a letter Hemingway wrote to Maxwell Perkins, in which he marvels at Markham's writing: "She has written so well, and marvelously well, that I was completely ashamed of myself as a writer" before noting that his memory of her was that she was a "high-grade bitch." That last part gets left off the cover blurb.)

The opening page of Beauvoir's *America Day by Day*, reissued by the University of California Press, alerts the reader that the publisher "gratefully acknowledges the contribution provided by the Literature in Translation Endowment Fund . . ." etc. In other words, a donation was required to bring us Simone de Beauvoir on the road.

I came upon the book during the years when I was taking multiple cross-country road trips around America and looking for writings from women who'd done the same—and not because they were running away, or being chased, or were out of options.

Beauvoir's description of leaving France for New York remains a favorite and one I return to regardless of my destination.

Something is about to happen. You can count the minutes in your life when something happens. Strokes of light sweep the ground, shining red and green; it's a gala evening, a late-night party—my party. . . . There. It's happened. I'm flying to New York. It's true. . . . I'm leaving my life behind. I don't know if it will be through anger or hope, but something is going to be revealed—a

world so full, so rich, and so unexpected that I'll have the extraordinary adventure of becoming a different me.

According to the plaque on the apartment building in Montparnasse, Beauvoir was in her forty-seventh year when she moved to this
building. The same age I will be in a few weeks. At the time, she was
in three relationships. Her lifelong partnership with Jean-Paul Sartre.
Her intense transatlantic affair with the American writer Nelson Al-
gren. And her seven-year relationship with French filmmaker Claude
Lanzmann, who was seventeen years her junior—twenty-seven to her
forty-four when they began. It was with Lanzmann that she shared a
ground-floor studio in this building.

Ellie finds me standing across the street from the plaque, leaning
against the brick wall of the Montparnasse cemetery (where Beauvoir
is buried) and staring up at the top floors of the building. Above the
four soaring windows is a terrace I can make out, which suggests
there is another floor above, though it's impossible to know for sure
from this angle.

"Look at those windows!" says Ellie. "I think I'd like that top one.
Imagine the view."

Do all women do this? Insert themselves in real estate as though
trying on an outfit. There is a Dorothy Parker short story I think
about often called "The Standard of Living," in which two young
working women stroll up Fifth Avenue window shopping. They are
playing their favorite game: Someone has died and left you a million
dollars. The stipulation is you spend it all on yourself. No one else
gets a penny. Their game is ruined when one takes up the other's dare
to go inside a jewelry store and inquire about a string of pearls she

has declared will be her first small purchase. The sticker shock—a quarter of a million—upends their belief in how far a million can get them and sends them silently running. But a few blocks later, they reinvent the game. What if someone left you $10 million?

No one is leaving Ellie or me any money. Neither of us has safety nets of any sort. Which does not keep us from walking around the corner to see the other side of the building, trying to assess the value of each floor. Ellie is guessing the price per square meter and googles the address to see if anything has been sold lately.

"€14,000 per meter! Actually, not terrible considering."

"What does that mean? How much would the whole apartment sell for?" I still don't understand how the French measure real estate.

"Hmm. Let's see. If it's like sixty-five square meters, like €850,000."

"What is sixty-five square meters?"

"Three times as large as my flat."

I decide it's a large one-bedroom. Not terrible. The same price as New York, except in New York the maintenance fees would be in the thousands and here they're in the hundreds or less.

"Someone named Lee Miller used to live here," says Ellie. "There's a petition to put up a plaque for her."

"Lee Miller the photographer?"

Ellie reads it in French and then translates: "It says, 'former model, who became an artist photographer then a correspondent for war during World War II. She marked her time as a figure of emancipated femininity,' whatever that means."

"It's probably another way of saying feminist. She was a fashion model who became a photographer, and then a war photographer," I tell Ellie. "She was at the liberation of some of the concentration camps. There's a very famous photo of her taking a bath in Hitler's bathtub." I pull it up to show Ellie. There is Miller, naked, age thirty-six, in Hitler's deep bathtub the same day he killed himself.

"She *should* have a fucking plaque," says Ellie, indignant.

Lee Miller is one of those figures who offers different things to different women. Lithe and blonde, she was plucked from the street, at age nineteen, by Condé Nast himself and transformed into a famous fashion model of the early twenties. Unsatisfied, she relocated to Paris where she tracked down the photographer Man Ray. Legend has it, she first encountered him on a staircase leading to a cellar bar popular with artists, and declared she was going to be his student. He brushed her aside and said he was traveling to Biarritz the next day for holiday. Unperturbed, she announced she was going with him, and did. Their affair lasted four years, during which time Miller became Ray's apprentice, sometime model, and collaborator. The solarization technique in photography is credited to both of them, though of the two, Miller seemed to be the only one who could explain in detail how the discovery happened. Ray was reportedly often furious that while they were together Miller took on other lovers, pursuing the sort of open relationships that men, including Ray, took for granted.

Later, during the war, Miller was employed as a photographer by *Vogue*, embedded with US forces as they made their way across Europe following the D-Day invasion, writing gruesome dispatches for *Vogue* to accompany her photographs.

More than the famous photo of Miller in Hitler's tub, or the ones taken of her by Man Ray, or the surrealist self-portraits she took, the photo I come back to most is one Miller took in Rennes in August

1944. She had just traveled there after filing a report in Saint-Malo. Saint-Malo is an ancient village on the coast of Bretagne that was occupied as an outpost for the Germans, and then flattened by the Allies. Completely flattened. If you go there today, every building you encounter is a reconstruction of what was once there. Like the Tiergarten in Berlin, which was stripped of every last shred of vegetation, down to blades of grass, by starving Berliners after Liberation. Miller arrived in Saint-Malo as the remaining Germans were trying to call a truce and offering to release the remaining French in their custody to safety. In a 1944 piece for *Vogue* Miller describes "old women, with bundles and dazed eyes, little hand-holding groups of girls, stumbling along . . . couples with babies, prams piled with all they had saved of their possessions . . . prim women, and nuns in immaculate white, and whores. A few were hoisted out of line by the police for their crimes, and a few trustworthy others kept at the bridgehead to help identify any possibly escaping Germans."

Miller later recounts her experience with a woman and her small children being held in the jail and interviewed by Allied counterintelligence for consorting with the Germans and aiding them. "Horizontal collaboration" was the term for it. In this woman's possession were receipts, and what Miller describes as pornographic photographs which "for some strange reason she clung to." It's not clear whether the photographs are of her.

"She made a pretty pose with her children when I wanted to photograph her," writes Miller.

The photograph that Miller takes a few days later in Rennes is of a group of four women, including perhaps this aforementioned "horizontal collaborator," who are being treated as Nazi collaborators. Their heads have been shaved as punishment for their consorting, and they are encircled by a large group of locals. Female collaborators were often marched through the streets after the public head-shaving ceremony. In this case, the attention of the crowd around these *femmes tondues* has been diverted away from the women, and upward toward Miller's camera. All but the women are grinning as Miller snaps her photo.

I think of those shaven women sometimes and wonder what their options were. Consorting in lieu of what, I wonder. Starvation? Rape? Or was the consortment in exchange for comfort. I have no idea. I've never been in a war zone, I've never starved. But Miller's tone in her dispatches makes abundantly clear that she, a woman tasked with observing, evinces no sympathy for the decisions made by these women about their bodies.

Miller didn't reemerge as a notable figure until sometime after her death in 1977, when her son discovered a cache of her wartime photographs; she never spoke of her experiences. And yet the fact this building held both her and Simone de Beauvoir, at different times, feels like an electric jolt. On the one hand, it's easy to say that Miller's "emancipated femininity" was just the sort of thing Beauvoir was writing about (after the fact). On the other hand, Miller, for all her extraordinariness, was first emancipated by her own beauty and then again by the fissure of war that allowed so many white women to briefly slip out of their roles before being strapped back down a few years later. It seems to me that in some ways it's the women Miller photographed, rather than Miller herself, that Beauvoir was writing toward.

Ellie is furiously tapping into her phone. I step back, trying to guess which apartment might have been Miller's. A ground-floor apartment?

The smaller top-floor artist studios? Beauvoir and Miller were only nine months apart in age, though it's difficult to imagine them occupying the same space, literal or otherwise. By the time Beauvoir moved to this address, Miller would have been in the English countryside, teaching herself to cook. Where Beauvoir spent the 1950s traveling and writing and intellectualizing her arguments, Miller disappeared into the domestic, attending Le Cordon Bleu and submitting her recipes to *Vogue*. Something about the structure of the kitchen presumably soothing the trauma of what she'd witnessed in the war.

Miller was not the only woman correspondent present at Dachau. Martha Gellhorn, one of the few journalists to participate in the D-Day invasion, was also there (she snuck on board a hospital ship after her soon-to-be ex-husband Ernest Hemingway stole her *Collier's* press credentials). As was twenty-three-year-old Marguerite Higgins, who was the first woman journalist to arrive there and would go on to make a name for herself covering the Korean War before dying while on assignment in the Vietnam War. All three filed separate dispatches. (Miller's story, for *Vogue*, was titled "Believe It.") Though I can find no record of them having met at Dachau, we know they must have. Somehow, somewhere, in that inner circle of hell they'd arrived at, their paths must have crossed. What would that conversation have been? What would those glances have said? I'd like to know.

The only record I can find of this group of extraordinary women interacting is from a little-known book published at the end of the last century titled *The Women Who Wrote the War* by Nancy Caldwell Sorel. In it Sorel recounts that, on their march across Germany with the liberating Allied army, Higgins shared a cottage outside Cologne with Miller and fellow journalist Helen Kirkpatrick, and that Higgins had the temerity to keep closing the windows at night despite the other, older journalists wanting them open. But there is little else to suggest community.

Ellie has apparently been applying her love of scholarship to our afternoon. "I've been looking up feminist plaques," she says, emerging from her phone. "We're not so far from Edith Wharton's house. Do you want to go there?"

Absolutely, I do. "Tour me, Ellie," I say. I experience so much of Paris directly on my own, it's fun to have someone else take the wheel. We leave Beauvoir and Miller behind and redirect ourselves toward the 6th.

Edith Wharton's sojourn in Paris was unknown to me until recently. During lockdown I'd reread *The Age of Innocence* for the first time since high school. So many scenes took my breath away: Newland Archer dropping down to kiss Ellen Olenska's shoe; Ellen Olenska's shutting of the drapes at the last minute; the divine experience of being fully submerged in another world. I'd gone digging through Google, trying to locate the square where the scene had taken place. What emerged instead was Wharton's Paris bio. She'd arrived in 1907, age forty-five, a year younger than I am now, at the tail end of an unhappy marriage to her husband, Teddy Wharton, and taken up residence in wealthy, established residences of the 7th, along Rue de Varenne, near where the Italian embassy is now located, down the street from the Musée Rodin. She was immediately welcomed in Paris by the same circles of money she had traversed in Boston and New York (and had written about so devastatingly in *The House of Mirth*, and then more benevolently in *The Age of Innocence*). Wharton became renowned both for her salons and her talent as a host. During the First World War, she shifted gears entirely and opened a workroom for unemployed women, as well as helped establish the American Hostels for Refugees and raised over $100,000 to support relief efforts. She even visited the front. After the war, she returned to America bemoaning the hordes of tourists that had taken over the city in the aftermath of the Armistice (the forever complaint of the expat . . . why are there so many of us here?).

Less known, or perhaps unknown except to Wharton scholars, is that shortly after her arrival in Paris, squarely in the middle-aged years, she began a heady affair with a man named William Morton Fullerton, an American print journalist. He was the great passion of Wharton's life. Her letters to Fullerton are imbued with the same abandon we associate with teenagers and first loves. She writes: "You more than anyone else have the power to make me happy. . . . I long for you with such an intensity of feeling that it almost makes me sink from exhaustion sometimes—you are ever present with me."

The affair lasted three years. Fullerton had a reputation for being a bit of a scoundrel; one acquaintance called him an "elegant seducer." But this did not diminish Wharton's experience. She later wrote: "I could take my life up again courageously if I only understood; for whatever those months were to you, to me they were a great gift, a wonderful enrichment; & still I rejoice & give thanks for them!"

(We only have these letters because Fullerton refused to destroy them per Wharton's request after the affair ended. She desperately did not want them scrutinized by prying eyes. Sorry, not sorry, Edith.)

I'm describing this all to Ellie as we arrive in front of Wharton's building, on a long, narrow street full of imposing buildings. One gets the sense that loitering is discouraged here.

Waiting for us is a large plaque. There is no question of this spot being marked. The first two lines of text read:

EDITH WHARTON

Romancière américaine

I ask Ellie what *romancière* means.

"Novelist."

"It makes it sound like she wrote romance novels," I say. "Which she did in a way, I suppose. The French really have a way of getting to the heart of the matter. Funny how I immediately think it's diminishing to her."

Ellie nods and translates the next line for me:

She was a first-rate American writer, who immigrated to France for the love of the country and literature.

Fair. The following is in English and French:

My years of Paris life were spent entirely in the rue de Varenne—rich years, crowded and happy years.

And then:

Proche de Henry James, l'oeuvre d'Edith Wharton met en scène d'un trait à la fois délicat et mordant, la bonne société dont elle est issue.

"Why is Henry James's name up there?" I ask Ellie. I wonder if I'm missing something in the translation.

"It says she was close to him and showed the high society from which she came, tenderly and bitingly at the same time."

"So, they mention him just so we know they knew each other? Not that he lived here too."

"It just means they were friends and colleagues."

I make a mental note to walk through Place de la Contrescarpe and see if Gertrude Stein factors into Hemingway's plaque that marks his home there. I'm guessing, no.

I try to imagine Wharton rushing through these doors, down across the river and to the corner of the Louvre to meet Fullerton for a clandestine rendezvous. How the world must have expanded for her at a time and age in the exact ways we are told it will be collapsing.

"You woke me from a long lethargy," she wrote to Fullerton after their affair ended. "A dull acquiescence in conventional restrictions, a needless self-effacement. If I was awkward & inarticulate it was because, literally, all one side of me was asleep."

In Wharton's papers after her death were found pages of a short story, titled "Beatrice Palmato," which can only be described as Whartonian erotica: "As his hand stole higher, she felt the secret bud of her body swelling, yearning, quivering hotly to burst into bloom. Ah, here was his subtle forefinger pressing it, forcing its tight petals softly apart." Wharton was clearly a woman who knew good sex. Some scholars think that in "Beatrice Palmato," she was writing about an incestuous relationship between a father and daughter, though this remains speculation. What is clear is Wharton's determination, at the height of middle age, to record in some way her own desire, her own pleasure, to get those experiences down on paper, even if that pleasure had to be redirected into the body of a young girl. Thinking of it now, I find myself wishing Wharton had instead given us the story of a grown woman who comes to Paris and emerges from her time here fully in the throes of not just her sexual powers but her mental ones. A woman in her prime. Portrait of another sort of Lady.

"This way," says Ellie, pointing back down Rue de Varennes in the direction we just came.

"Who's next?" I ask.

"Romy Schneider lived around the corner from here."

"From here?"

"Yes, this way." Ellie begins to read to me from her phone. "Romy Schneider was a French *actrice*, born in 1938. She first came to fame playing the character Sissi . . ."

Oh, I know who Romy Schneider is.

This past May, not long after it first reopened to the public, Film Forum in New York began a short run of *La Piscine*, the 1969 film Romy Schneider did with her former real-life lover Alain Delon, which also co-starred a young Jane Birkin. When the run first started, New York was still limiting audience size: in a theater that could fit one hundred, only twenty-five people were allowed.

I bought my first ticket to *La Piscine* on the recommendation of my friend Marisa. We'd been to see *Rear Window* a week earlier, during which the sold-out crowd of twenty-five had basically laughed at every line out of the pure joy of being in the room together. When the trailer for *La Piscine* came on, Marisa, a person renowned for her exquisite taste, leaned over and said, "You must see it." Beautiful people, blue water. I didn't need much convincing. It was scheduled to be in the theater for only a week. I went alone to the first Saturday afternoon show expecting nothing. Which, plotwise, is initially what I got: *La Piscine* is so slow moving, the players so beautiful, the colors so vibrant, it felt like slipping into a pool, something I'd barely been able to do for more than a year. Alain Delon, the Brad Pitt of his day (or perhaps, Brad Pitt is the Alain Delon of our day), and the gorgeous Romy Schneider play Jean-Paul and Marianne, two lovers *en vacances* in the South of France. They are visited by Harry, Marianne's former lover and Jean-Paul's former mentor (so French), and Harry's daughter Penelope, played by a young, wide-eyed Jane Birkin. Very little happens for about two hours. They swim. They make love. Delon makes suggestive moves toward Birkin, while Schneider remains serene. Schneider wears a backless green Courrèges dress to dinner. She gives new meaning to Oxford shirts. Her bathing suits are their own characters. They throw a party, and everyone comes. Schneider lies on the couch after a day of relaxation and says, "Tomorrow, I will take a long siesta."

Eventually, off camera, Delon and Birkin's characters consummate their relationship. "The first swim is always tiring," Schneider says to Birkin in reference to the virginity Birkin's character has just lost to Delon. Schneider tells Delon he is free to do what he wants. And then Delon kills Harry. The last half hour of the movie involves a cover-up, and a police detective, seemingly on loan from a Pink Panther film. Schneider in another beautiful Courrèges dress. The end.

I could not get enough. The luxury. The sensuality. The colors. The indulgence. I bought a second ticket the minute I arrived home. I wanted to live in that pool with those beautiful people who planned their long siestas. Back I went, again and again. I tried to move into the film. I wanted to float slowly away. During one showing I sat behind a pair of older women. At the ninety-minute mark one turned to the other and said in a loud voice, "Can you believe there's another *hour* of this?"

The plot itself seemed inconsequential to me. It was the languishing. The beautiful languishing. The skin rubbing against skin. The blue water. The slowness. I spent a full week online trying to source a bathing suit similar to Romy Schneider's black Courrèges. I sunk into the film so many times, I began to effortlessly pick up on all the subtle imagery and hints. The way Delon pretends to drown Schneider in the opening scenes. The emphasis on the watch. The undertones of incest between Harry and Birkin's Penelope.

The run was extended a week at a time. Each time I'd return home and snap up a ticket before it closed. And then it was extended again. And then again. Every time I went, the theater was a bit more crowded. I was not the only one looking to succumb to a slow if slightly menacing world. One time I sat down, and the young man in front of me turned around and said with intense glee, "Isn't it just so amazing that we're all here together?!"

There is no plaque marking Romy's building. Constructed in the 1960s, the building doesn't match the style of the rest of the neighborhood and is a bit of an eyesore. It's difficult to know if this was the building Schneider had actually lived in, or if this building replaced something after she left. We walk around inspecting all the corners to make sure we're not missing anything. We're not.

"Well, that's a disappointment," says Ellie.

There's no satisfaction in learning about Schneider's real life either. Her son died after impaling himself on a fence he was trying to climb over at age fourteen. In the aftermath, she drank herself, if not to death, then right up close to it, dying at age forty-three. Knowing this, one wonders if part of the magic of *La Piscine* is that it managed to capture all its stars at the height of their power.

As it was with Beauvoir and Miller, Schneider's proximity to Wharton's house is fascinating to me. There is of course no way they would have crossed paths, except on a library shelf. But there is something electric in understanding the literal connection of their geography. These small islands of women's lives we cleave to, but that are never seemingly connected to one another in the understanding of our history. And yet, here they are, in such close proximity.

We're going to visit Colette next. But she's across the river and we decide we need sustenance in order to get there. We stop at Café de Flore, famed for its history of attracting iconic artists and writers, and sit at an outside table. Were Café de Flore your only measurement of Paris right now, you would think the city was more crowded than it actually is. Nearly every table is occupied. Perhaps every tourist left in Paris is here right now. I order a *chocolat chaud* and Ellie has a *chantilly*. In my highly researched opinion, the Café de Flore *chocolat chaud* is the best in Paris, perhaps the world.

It isn't merely served to you either. Rather, it is *presented*. First the table is set with a circular paper cover with an illustration of Café de Flore, and Paris in the background. Then two small water glasses with CAFÉ DE FLORE printed on them are set down. Then *une carafe d'eau*. Finally, the *garçon*, in his white shirt and green vest, emerges, tray laden and held aloft, and down from its heights is delivered a small jug containing the thick chocolate drink. Then a cup and saucer, with a spoon on one side, and two carefully wrapped sugar cubes on the other that seem to me to be the *chocolat chaud* version of butter being delivered with a charcuterie plate.

Ellie's *chantilly* arrives with a glass of whipped cream—*chantilly*—and an extra spoon with which to administer it. The chocolate pours out thickly and slowly, how I imagine the river of chocolate in Willy Wonka's factory would be. You must drink it both quickly and slowly. Consuming small portions, one sip at a time, but continuously so that you reach the end before the contents of the jug get cold. It's not for the faint of heart (or stomach).

We watch the waiter emerge again and again with tray after tray of *chocolat chaud*. Each tray must weigh at least five pounds. Down come the glasses and the carafes and the jugs and cups and saucers. I wonder if he has nightmares of drowning in rivers of *chocolat chaud*, like the Oompa Loompas swept away. Scrubbing off the smell of it every night the way I did cigarette smoke way back when I waited tables before the smoking ban.

We pay eight euros each for our drinks—with that price comes the promise that we could sit here for as long as we want, should we so choose—and make our way through the streets that lead to the river. From here, it feels like a normal August in Paris. The people who own these flats are never here this month—at least I've never seen them. The art galleries are always closed. Colette's home is across the river in the Palais Royal.

"There better be a fucking plaque," says Ellie, increasingly indignant at the absence of markings of women's lives. Her indignance feels bracing to me. A reminder we deserve visibility. That said . . .

"I don't think anyone in France is forgetting about Colette," I say.

The Palais Royal, as the name suggests, was once a palace. It sits opposite the Louvre (also a former palace) smack in the middle of the 1st arrondissement. Paris is as subject to the shifting appeal of neighborhoods as any other major city, and while the circular nature of the arrondissement layout can be confusing at first, there is never any doubt the 1st is so designated because of its place at the top of the cultural and moneyed food chain. The courtyard of the Palais Royal is now a public garden with manicured trees, the ground-floor arcade now shops. Walking through the narrow pass, off an equally dark and narrow street, and into the sunlit center can feel a bit like entering the secret garden. If the secret garden had once been occupied by royalty.

Colette moved to her apartment here in 1927 at the age of fifty-four, three years after her marriage to her second husband collapsed following her affair with her sixteen-year-old stepson, Bertrand de Jouvenel. That affair was the basis for her novels *Chéri* and *The End of Chéri*, about Léa, an aging courtesan, and her love affair with a much younger man named Chéri, who marries a woman his own age and eventually leaves Léa.

Colette stayed at the Palais Royal for the rest of her life, including through the Second World War, during which she wrote for Nazi publications. She was nursed into old age by her third husband, a Jewish man named Maurice Goudeket, who was sixteen years her junior.

The character Léa is forty-nine when the novel *Chéri* begins, six years into her love affair with Chéri, which began when he was nineteen (presumably a more acceptable age than sixteen).

At forty-nine years old, Léonie Vallon, known as Léa de Lonval, was ending a successful career as a well-paid courtesan and obliging girl who had been spared life's flattering catastrophes and noble griefs. She kept her birth date a secret; but she freely admitted, letting fall on Chéri a look of voluptuous condescension, that she was reaching the age where she was due some small pleasures.

Colette had been spared neither life's catastrophes nor noble griefs. She was a writer, not a courtesan. Her first books, the Claudine series, had been spectacular bestsellers. Though the books were written by Colette, they were published under her first husband's pen name, Willy. He retained the copyright long after their divorce, sending Colette to perform on stage at music halls to make a living.

Colette was a French icon by the time she died in 1954. There is no question that there will be a plaque marking her presence. Her grave in Père Lachaise Cemetery is piled high with pens, as is custom on graves of French writers (Marguerite Duras's, in Montparnasse, is similarly adorned). And sure enough, there it is. A small gold plaque, slightly weathered with age—this was not a delayed recognition—at the north end of the *parc*, just to the left of the arched entrance leading back out onto another narrow street.

Chéri came out in 1920, the year Edith Wharton left Paris and the year before Hemingway arrived. When you google "Did Hemingway ever meet Colette" or "Did Hemingway ever meet Edith Wharton," the only result that comes close to connecting these names is a blog entry on a Harry Potter fan site about how J. K. Rowling's favorite books growing up were the Claudine series and the ways this may have manifested in the depiction of Hogwarts.

Surely, if Colette and Hemingway had met, one of them would have recorded it. If Beryl Markham was a "high-grade bitch," and Gertrude Stein was "a bitch is a bitch is a bitch"—which is how Hemingway inscribed a copy of *Death in the Afternoon* to her after she called him "yellow"—one can only imagine what Hemingway's impression of Colette might have been. Perhaps nothing. Perhaps silence because Colette would have eaten him up and spit him out.

It's the connection between Colette and Wharton that fascinates me. The looser social restrictions Wharton was after when she relocated to Paris are so deeply embodied in Colette and her novels. Did they ever even casually cross paths? Were they ever asked about one another?

And yet, it is also through Colette I find some of the female collision I've been craving. For instance, Lee Miller photographed both Martha Gellhorn and Colette, within a year of each other, no less. The former in 1943, before either had set off to cover the invasion, and the latter in Paris in November 1944, presumably after Miller had returned from the front. Imagine being a fly on the wall in either of those sessions. Miller and Gellhorn particularly had followed a similar life trajectory from wealthy upbringing to glamorous women to war reporting and must have at least reflected on some of their shared experiences. But not surprisingly, it is Colette for whom the juiciest interaction with Gellhorn is reserved. Or at least the juiciest we know about.

In her twenties Gellhorn had a long, impassioned affair with Co-

lette's stepson, Bertrand de Jouvenel (he was an adult at this point). At
some point Gellhorn and Colette met, which we know about from a
letter Gellhorn later wrote in 1993 to the author Donna Tartt (talk
about secret history). Gellhorn described their meeting thusly:

> She was a terrible woman. Absolute, utter hell. She hated me on
> first sight. She was lying on a chaise-longue like an odalisque,
> with green shadow on her cat's eyes and a mean, bitter little
> mouth. She kept touching her frizzy hair, which was tinted with
> henna . . . Having looked me over maliciously, she insisted that I
> pencil in my eyebrows—which were so blonde as to be non-
> existent—using a black crayon, so that the lines almost met in the
> middle. Well, I did it. Why? Because she told me to. And it was
> three days before some kind friend said to me, "My dear, what
> dreadful thing have you done to your face?" She was jealous of
> me . . . and Bertrand adored her all his life. He never understood
> when he was in the presence of evil.

Colette was a whole other sort of high-grade bitch, it seems.
Though by the time Gellhorn wrote this, she was in her eighties, going
blind, and was by all accounts not the easiest companion herself.
Meanwhile, Colette's love of remaking other people's faces once manifested in an actual business. In the midthirties she opened a beauty salon
in Paris where she sold products that she made herself with fruits,
vegetables, and cold cream. For the packaging, she used her own profile; for the label she used her signature. The business was a raging
failure—she was accused of making one young client look like a so-
called streetwalker—but Colette as the original beauty influencer

who once remade Martha Gellhorn is something I dearly wish we could hear more about.

We also know that Colette and Josephine Baker knew one another, and not casually. In a 1936 letter addressed to Baker, Colette writes: "You send me a whole garden of flowers. In exchange, take my loving memory . . ." and signs it "Your old friend, Colette." They clearly had a friendship (and possibly more, according to some). And yet, to find out even this you have to dig.

We can't check on the plaque status of Josephine Baker; during her career she lived in the suburb Le Vésinet twenty minutes to the west of Paris, and later relocated to Château des Milandes in the South. But this seems somewhat moot for a change as her image is everywhere. Entire tour packages have been constructed around Baker's time in France. Like Wharton, she also endeared herself to the French during the War (World War II in this case), working as a spy for the French resistance. After the war, when she was in her forties, she adopted twelve children and raised them at Milandes. And yet, it is only this fall, according to a news item I saw, fifty years after her death, that she will be honored with a tomb in the Pantheon, France's secular temple and monument to their "great men." She is only the sixth woman to be included and the first Black woman.

We know so much about Fitzgerald and Hemingway—the sharpness, generosity, and cruelty of that friendship (if it can be called that). We know about the friendships with James Joyce.

We know the stories of the young women who come to Paris looking for transformation. The Sabrinas. The Sally Jay Gorces. The Emilys. They are so connected they blur together until it's difficult to tell one from the other.

And yet, we know these other women—the passionate middle-age Wharton; the elder Colette in her prime; Beauvoir and her young lover—only as prickly iconoclasts. Isolated from each other, a story unto themselves, and therefore hard to repeat or have commonality with in any way. I have to search them out and be surprised each time when I find in them some shard of my own reflection.

I never know whether it's rage inducing or a relief, the sensation that you are not alone. It's often both at the same time. Why am I required to look for this commonality in the first place? Why has this feast of connected history not been served up to me regularly? Carted out, over and over, like the *chocolat chauds*. Thick and rich and popular and full of ceremony.

I tell Ellie she should start offering a weekend tour called "Why Isn't There a Fucking Plaque?"

"God, there must be so many," says Ellie. "I've lived here for nearly a decade and didn't know most of this until today. It's infuriating."

In our afternoon together, we have cobbled together just a handful of examples. A scattering of stars that shine specifically to me. That I can, if I focus on them, construct in a shape like a constellation, which I can use to navigate my life by, like seafarers of old. That I can also point to others, and say, You're hardly the first one here. See that? Go that way.

But what would a galaxy look like? What if we mapped all the stars, the ones that I don't even know are there, or sometimes that I don't even know I should be looking for? And then when you do find them, you think, How have I gone this long without knowing this was here? How differently might I have steered my life if I had? The assumption must be that they are there, have been all along. We need better maps. I shouldn't have to look this hard. No one should. That's where the anger comes from. I shouldn't have to look this hard to know I am not alone. Not the first. Not original. I shouldn't be dependent on the random placement of plaques or a casting director's decision to cast a forty-year-old woman to see some element of my life, or its potential, in one that existed before me, fictional or otherwise. I should be able to see it as clearly and easily as I can see the night sky just by looking up.

Le Chiot Italian

The unabashed energy of the twenty-seven-year-old Italian with the flowing hair and beard bounds through the phone like a puppy let loose. I can't help but be charmed by it. No pretense. No innuendo. He is intrigued, he tells me. He is dazzled. His profile photos look like templates for covers of paperback romance novels you'd find at the airport. His persistence charms me. He is leaving Paris soon but wants to reroute his trip to the airport to come and see me. His willingness to risk missing his flight drops me back into that young mind that believes every new experience one is having is new to everyone. High-stakes living. It's noon. His flight is in five hours. I tell him to come over.

He arrives sweaty and apologetic for being so. I find myself immediately sliding into the role of the confident, assured comforter. "It's fine," I say. "Don't worry, it's just sweat." I can tell part of the thrill of me to him is his own willingness to risk coming here.

He looks exactly like his photos. Better, even.

He looks at me the way I imagine the fabulists envisioned young girls being regarded by wolves before they are eaten.

Careful hands on the buttons of my shirt become less careful.

Off come the clothes. Round go his eyes. (What big eyes you have, I want to say). He remains dazzled—something that continues to give me a jolt so ingrained is the habit of only seeing my own physical flaws. He begins whispering in what I assume is Italian, but really does not need translation. The me, now naked, that emerges in the face of all this energy and excitement is calm. Confident. I hear myself say what I want without having to think about how to articulate it. No hand-holding. This, I imagine, is what is attractive. I consider how, when I was his age, my sense of pleasure was entirely centered on making sure the other person experienced it. I did not know what I liked. How could I have? What do young women do now, with so much more knowl-edge available to them about how bodies work and what women like better? Do they wield it or are they minced by it?

I can tell immediately what sort of porn the Italian prefers by the way he tries to position himself. Position me. But he asks first about everything. Is this okay? Is that? It is all okay.

As much as I rage against the age machine that I feel I'm relent-lessly being fed into by culture, I cannot deny the appeal of the youn-ger body. The taut skin. The thick hair. The *energy*. So much energy. And the simple desire to please me. Which he does. Several times.

I wouldn't be twenty-seven again for anything. So little about it was enjoyable. But this adjacency to it is so pleasurable I can only be grateful I knew enough to say yes to it.

ELEVEN

The Young Women

When Greta Garbo was thirty-five, she retired from Hollywood and eventually disappeared into a seven-room apartment in the Campanile building in Manhattan, located on 52nd Street, where it meets the East River. This is where she remained until her death. The living room of her fifth-floor home boasted spectacular views of the 59th Street Bridge and, across the river, the neon Pepsi-Cola sign in Queens, the latter of which was later presided over by fellow actress Joan Crawford, who once said of Garbo, "One almost feels grateful to Garbo for keeping herself so resolutely to herself, for leaving us a little mystery."

For the decades that followed her retirement, Garbo, as women often do, grew in our imagination in her silence. She became a silhouette of herself, capturing the public's imagination as she sliced through the Manhattan streets in her trench coat and sunglasses and headscarf. A walking mystery. Wikipedia will tell you that sightings of her became a sort of "city sport." When I read that, I think of rare animals who sometimes make their home in Central Park—coyotes, bald eagles, a snow owl, an exotic duck—and capture the city's devotion in their willingness to walk among us as avatars of singular otherness.

"I want to be alone," Garbo is quoted ad nauseam as saying (she later insisted what she actually said was, "I want to be *let* alone.").

Garbo was rarely, actually, alone. She had a vibrant social life, and extensive walking companions. She had the city. Wikipedia will also tell you it was a life of simplicity (as one can expect in a seven-room Sutton Place apartment, naturally) and leisure.

I thought of Garbo sometimes during lockdown, on the days the city was especially empty, though never as empty as the photos wanted you to believe. At its emptiest, New York just felt like the sun was rising at an incorrect hour. The movement on the streets familiar to anyone who has done overnight shift work. In photos, Garbo seems like a blur on the streets, intimately anonymous in the crowds. I felt myself a blur on my bike, anonymous in the absence of crowds.

On Instagram from time to time, much like Didion's packing list, floats by Garbo's response to a dinner invitation: "Thank you for thinking of me, and I am sorry, but for the moment, I can speak to no one." Its appeal, I think, is in its directness. A woman not invested in making excuses or other people comfortable. Even the apology feels like an exercise in self-respect.

The other quote from Garbo I often see is her explanation for ignoring a dinner invitation with Gloria Swanson. "There was no one to make me."

No one knows for sure why Garbo retired when she did, but the general sense is that some part of it was because she felt she had aged out of

Hollywood. Or rather, she was in fear of her imminent aging out. "Time leaves traces on our small faces and bodies," she said shortly before retiring. "It's not the same anymore, being able to pull it off." It's not hard, even now, to see her, caught between the specters of her encroaching age and the youth emerging behind her. There is always youth emerging—triumphant, powerful, unquestioned, full of potential.

My first memory of youth emerging was the trailer for *National Lampoon's European Vacation*. Chevy Chase and his family are driving down a highway, his pleasant wife beside him, when he looks out the window and spots a gorgeous blonde in a sports car pulling alongside. (I was too young to know it was Christie Brinkley, or even the significance of that. I only knew that she looked just like my Barbie dolls.) Her smile blinds. His eyes go boing. His wife is oblivious. Oblivious and boring.

The year before I moved to New York, a film called *The First Wives Club* exploded at the box office. I was twenty-two and it held exactly zero interest for me. If anything, the trailer—which still exists in my mind's eye as featuring three overdressed middle-aged women, marching through a department store, laden with shopping bags, cackling—elicited mild contempt. Wherever those women lived, I had no intention of going. They are, of course, the first wives who've been left for younger women, living it up on their ex-husband's dime. Vengeful. Sarah Jessica Parker is the younger woman. Or one of them.

Years later, Sarah Jessica Parker was cast in *Sex and the City*, where she plays Carrie, a woman in her thirties whose seasons-long love interest, Big, refuses to commit to her but then immediately marries the twenty-something Natasha shortly after meeting her.

I could go on, obviously, but why even bother compiling a list. It's an impossible task. Culturally speaking, man leaves wife for younger woman is not news. It is un-news. It is the norm. It is more than the norm. It is the air that we breathe. It is the blood in our veins.

Sandra messages me to see if I want to meet her and Marcel in Parc Monceau. I had told her I might be headed up there. I visit *parcs* in Paris the way one might visit people, and I hadn't seen Monceau since my first week here. Maybe there are so few stories about pleasure because so little happens. How many pages can you spend describing languishing before it's like, Great, bring on the emergency. Where's the action? Inciting incident, please! And yet, this is how many of my days are filled. Paris seems to encourage sitting. For the most part pleasure is a mood, not a narrative. It exists in the memory as a feeling you want to return to. The sun. The sound of water. The afternoons in the park that are so similar they blend together.

I tell Sandra I'll be up there within the hour.

It's a warm day. Paris in August normally gets a handful of truly hot days and this seems to be one of them. It's on these days I miss iced coffee. Over the years little tentacles of American living have stretched across the ocean into Paris. You wouldn't necessarily think iced coffee—big plastic cups jammed with cubes, poured over with regular coffee and then milk—is an American thing, but it was only recently that I could visit my family outside Toronto and say "iced coffee" and not get handed something that looked like a blended coffee slushy, so sweet my teeth felt like they were dislocating from my jaw with every sip. And lately it has emerged in Paris.

There are only one or two places in Paris I know of where I can get a *café glacé, à emporter* even. One's in the Marais and one's in the 11th, a ten-minute walk from me. I decide to route my trip up and over to the 8th past it. This café is on a square, and it's less like traditional French cafés and more like the coffee shops in New York. There are no tables inside. It's a nod to how much the 11th has changed in the last decade; gentrification is slower here, but it marches on. You order at the counter, where there is a small case of baked goods, and then move down to the other room where the coffee gets made. This is only one of two locations in the city, but they have a branded cookbook, carefully photographed. It sits on a shelf alongside the coffee bar with espresso pots and presses (are they also called French presses in France? I don't actually know) that are for sale. There is a sign at the counter that says no computers on weekends (to interfere with the *convivialité*). My *café glacé* comes in a small, narrow paper cup. It's a shot of espresso, another shot of milk, and four ice cubes. The constant reminder the French prize control and discipline. I could slurp it down in about fifteen seconds but I don't.

At the tables outside, everyone strikes me as young and good-looking. My eyes settle on a long, handsome man with a beard and espadrilles reading and drinking coffee alone at a table in the sun. He looks appealing. I contemplate asking if I can join him, but as I emerge he closes his book, stands, and walks away. He is not as tall as he appears sitting down, and his round face somehow belies the seriousness of his first impression. The young woman who took my order immediately comes out and rearranges the chairs so they both face out to the street like sentinels, and then wipes the tables down. When she walks past, I can get a whiff of the acrid cleaning solution. She is slight, the way white French women often are. With fluffy blonde hair that's been tied back. She has a very French face, sharp bones, an extraordinary nose; it looks like the face of a peasant from a Millet painting. So striking. You must go through life knowing who you are with a face like that.

The truth is I haven't exactly been doing nothing. I was hired at the beginning of the summer to send out a weekly newsletter for a women-centric co-working space. The premise being something like, how to feel motivated, though the guidance was loose. It's only a five-month gig, but the money is just enough to cover some bills. Instead of writing pieces about working, I kept writing variations on the theme of the Google Calendar alert I would get every day that said "You have no events scheduled today." I don't get any complaints.

I'd also filed a story for the *New York Times* on the surprising success of *La Piscine* at Film Forum in New York.

Jane Birkin owns a corner of Instagram, but it is Romy Schneider, eight years her senior, who owns that film. A woman fully occupying her entire self. "Isn't she a revelation!?" messaged a friend after I posted a series of shots of the screen taken from my midrow seat.

There have been multiple remakes of *La Piscine*. Less "remakes" than "inspired by," but the contours are the same. I'd watched two of them as research for the *Times* piece. The 2003 film *Swimming Pool* starring Charlotte Rampling, and the 2015 film *A Bigger Splash* starring Tilda Swinton and Ralph Fiennes. In each case there is a beautiful younger woman, and in each case she is dealt with by the older woman with a degree of understanding and tolerance. In *A Bigger Splash*, Tilda Swinton is all sympathy and patience in the face of

Dakota Johnson's hostile beauty. In *Swimming Pool*, Charlotte Rampling is furious that her quiet has been interrupted but, in the end, takes charge of the calamity the gorgeous young woman has created. (That said, my favorite scene in *Swimming Pool* is Rampling wolfing down enormous bowls of yogurt that are clearly part of her strict life routine, one of the more honest depictions I've seen of how women eat alone.) In both cases, it is clear the power does not lie with youth.

I arrive at Monceau at the same time as Sandra, and we plant ourselves in dappled shade below one of the trees. Marcel is wearing a red neck scarf. He immediately lies down, rolls onto his back, and thrusts his paws in the air, shooting both of us do-you-see-my-belly looks.

Sandra is wearing a black taffeta skirt with a belt and large, dark sunglasses, which, once we sit in the shade, she perches on her head in a way that makes them appear to be the perfect accessory. She looks around and points out the dogs she recognizes. Once we were sitting in Montmartre having coffee and a dog came up to Marcel, and when they left, Sandra said, "Funny, I don't know that dog."

"Do you know all the dogs in Paris?" I asked her.

"Not all of them," she had responded seriously.

Sandra tells me her twenty-three-year-old neighbor, Emily, and one of Emily's friends might be joining us. In addition to all the dogs of Montmartre, Sandra seems to know all the young women who live there too.

"I had no one else to talk to!" she exclaims when I point this out.

"We couldn't leave the neighborhood. And it was comforting to have other people close by I could see. The age difference didn't seem to matter."

A few minutes later two slight, brunette young women with glowing skin and shirts tied around their waistbands appear. Between them walks a small dog. I immediately clock their attributes the way I clock my own deficiencies: without thought. The small, perky breasts. The smooth necks. The narrow upper arms. And then I automatically stack these up in their favor. Even as I wonder, What was being stacked up in my favor at that age that I was unaware I possessed.

Seconds after being introduced to both women—one is Emily and the other Naomi—I lose track of which name belongs to which girl. Which I shouldn't. They are not interchangeable. But they seem to me to be in some way flattened by their youth, the way the elderly are flattened by their age. Together, they vibrate as though they are thoroughbreds who've been removed from their stalls and brought out to the races.

I do know—from earlier conversations with Sandra—that one of them is sleeping with an older man. Or an older man is paying for her travel (she had told Sandra at one point that this scenario made her feel "powerful," which I suppose I can hardly fault her for feeling, when I still have friends who complain when a man doesn't pick up the check on the first date). And one of them has parents in the South who are footing the bill.

Their dog sniffs around and anxiously tries to make friends with Marcel. But Marcel is a rescue from a former French colony somewhere in the Indian Ocean, and has no interest in rejoining the ranks of dogs. Marcel is a dog who understands his bread has quite fortuitously been thickly buttered by humans and intends to remain as close to them as possible. Marcel is no fool, he knows good behavior will get him everywhere. He does not bark. He does not growl. He steers clear of other dogs.

Emily or Naomi spots my fluttering manuscript. "Are you a writer?"

"I am," I say.

"I'm a writer too."

There is no getting away from certain conversations.

"Amazing," I say, assuming she probably writes for somewhere. There are a lot of places to write for these days. "Where do you write for?"

She removes a thick journal from her bag; across the front of it in sparkly letters is printed *Emily*. One problem solved. I am talking to Emily. And Emily's journal is the size of a manuscript. "I'm a poet," she says. "I also journal. I'm too scared to read it to anyone, but I try to do it every day. I also write and I paint."

The temptation to stamp down, with my bylines and my publishing history, her simple statement, and along with it, blow away the potential of . . . time? Future? that surrounds her like a cloud, washes up against me. The temptation that follows—to use her to remind *myself* that I am, in fact, the real deal, is even stronger.

But I don't. I push it back. If there have been any lessons I've taken from aging, or taken from so much solitude, or from months of people posting photos of themselves on beaches and in country houses, it's that it's not actually all that difficult to be kind. Instead, I remind myself I, too, was once a writer who wrote only in journals. The difference being, I would never have conceived of calling myself a writer until I had actually been published somewhere, *let alone* produced a journal as evidence of my writing. It wasn't until my words were in print, by what I considered to be a reputable publication, that I felt I finally had the permission to call myself a writer. And getting words in print when I was coming up was *hard*, I remind myself. There were limited places and unforgiving gatekeepers. Perhaps the greatest writing success of my midtwenties was writing captions for the letters to the editor page of Tina Brown's *Talk* magazine, for free as a far-too-old-to-be-an-intern intern.

It is only when thoughts like these fly through my head that I finally feel my age. Complaining that someone didn't earn their dues? In a world that is finally full of a whole array of voices? *Good god.*

What I'm really struck by is Emily's, I'm not sure it's confidence, exactly, but the absence of shame. The willingness to be seen. But maybe there's no being unseen for this generation.

"Amazing," I eventually say again, struggling to be supportive. "I don't know the first thing about poetry."

Emily nods. She does not seem to require my attempted kindness or approval. "I've just moved to this new apartment, so I'm still trying to create the emotional space for myself where I'm able to create. It's hard. It's difficult to make adjustments. But I'm trying to show myself grace, and just be kind to myself."

This is actually what she says. And she means it. So many times, when Sandra has recounted some of her conversations with her younger neighborhood set, we stop her and say, "Is that actually what they said?" The answer is always yes. The mainstreaming of so-called therapy speak is both amusing and confusing. Sandra told me earlier that before Emily comes over, she always asks if Sandra has the emotional bandwidth for Emily's presence. Now I'm getting to experience this firsthand.

But I also infer another meaning: Emily has wealthy parents. She must be the one whose parents are expats in the South and who have allowed her to come up here and stay in their Paris apartment. I think about my first time in Paris. I was nineteen and had spent the year on my own, living and working in Europe. I'd left home immediately following high school and the trip was funded entirely by me. I'm never sure whether the fact I made only two phone calls to my parents the entire time is a measure of my relationship with them, or of the time (email didn't exist; long-distance phone calls were expensive). For much of my life this independence was something I was proud of, but increasingly I just think it's not a show of weakness to have support.

At the same time, I also think of all the things Emily is required to carve emotional space out of and from. I think of all my selves being split up over the last year, and then I look at this young woman, twenty-three years old, and how all her selves have been split up too. Not by isolation, but by too much connection. Too much knowledge. The way that the internet has robbed her of discovery. Of being allowed to *not* know, to have to find out on your own. The understanding of self being the result of the work of acquiring that knowledge. Instead, she has been raised in a funhouse, with every version of what life could look like reflected back to her.

And still, I want to hear more about the creation of emotional space. I wonder if this is what alien encounters feel like. I do sometimes feel like I'm conversing with another species entirely, which, maybe I am. It seems impossible social media has not rewired brains.

Naomi gets up to leave. The dog needs to be fed. I watch her walk away and think, She is a postcard for the French Girl. But I am a postcard too, to many people, I suppose.

185

"Writing is hard work," I say to Emily.

Emily explains her plans for the next few weeks. The city feels very loud and overwhelming right now, she tells me. "It's difficult to focus."

"Really?" I say, thinking how I'd barely had to pause at a round-about on my bike ride up here there was so little traffic.

This is something else I wonder at quite a lot. Do any of them have fun? Is fun even possible anymore? . . . I want to say. I'm assuming the answer is yes, even if I feel like every encounter I have with a person under the age of thirty is riddled with paralyzing anxiety (theirs, not mine). It's a different fun. It's their fun. I spent my twenties working in an old bar in New York where all the customers never passed over an opportunity to tell me I'd missed out on the best New York. Now I tell everyone they missed out on nineties New York (the last great New York). There is nothing new under the sun, etc. Maybe this really is just age. Maybe this is my version of the older women who find me dislikable. I get their dislike; Emily gets my pity. Maybe I'm alien to her.

"I've been out in the countryside this whole time," Emily says. "I just feel like I can't move here. And I can't think. It's amazing that you write. I'm really hopeful I will be able to again. If it's okay with you, I will write about today."

"Of course," I say, surprised by this. "You should write about anything you want."

"I just don't want you to feel I've appropriated you in any way."

I don't know how to respond to this. It feels like she is asking permission to exist as a thinking person in the world. And maybe she is. The concept of boundaries seems to have gone into overdrive to balance out all the connecting.

186

However much she fascinates me, Emily is not the voice of a generation (that conceit is a creation of the white man). She is a privileged young white woman who seems very sweet. And probably feels as though she has just as many problems as anyone else, just as I do, even if they are very different problems.

According to almost every single story we're told, I should feel envious of Emily. The youth. The potential. The luxury of the paid apartment. It's so ingrained. And yet, that envy feels like a phantom limb I'm supposed to possess, that I expect to find, and then don't. But still, I go searching for it.

It's not just Emily. Increasingly, I find I am almost entirely devoid of envy. After a lifetime of being encouraged to covet, it's the strangest sensation. How am I supposed to feel when I'm not left wanting. And I'm never more aware of it than when I'm face to face with the thing I'm supposed to be coveting the most: youth. Is this the result of leading the life I know I'm supposed to be leading? Or of the time we're living in? Probably some combination. I would not want to be one day younger than I am now. I wake up every day grateful that I did not have the internet in my youth. I remember life without the internet, and the full horror of life with it feels apparent to me every day. I wouldn't hand over my eighties childhood for a lifetime of smooth skin and perky breasts.

At the root of my fascination, though, lies the knowledge that had I made different decisions, Emily could be my daughter. Not my I-got-knocked-up-as-a-teenager daughter either. I'm twice her age. She's twenty-three years younger than me. I have cousins with children her age. If she had been my child, I'm aware I'd be bridging this gap in an entirely different way. That I'd likely be insisting she check in regularly.

That I'd want all the connection that from a distance I see as weakness. That the alien nature of her life would feel more appropriate. My mother's life also felt like it existed on a different planet than mine (I could not conceive of a childhood without television). This is probably how it should be.

Perhaps in the end it's the ways in which our lives overlap that make her seem so strange. She and I still have access to the same, if not dating, then sexual pool (for lack of a better term). My parents didn't understand how to work the VCR, whereas I, too, exist on the internet. Time was flattening even before lockdown temporarily erased it.

Instead of envy, all I can muster is sympathy, which is maybe not any more helpful than my grandparents' contempt for how "spoiled" I was (by plumbing and electricity, presumably). It smacks of condescension and irresponsibility, as if we are not both equally tied to this world we occupy. Still, I cannot shake the sense that it's my job to help these younger women I encounter manage their way through raging waters as best I can. To learn to swim better. These waters are only going to get rougher for you, I think. I'm here to assist.

In theory.

Emily walks with us back to the Blanche Métro stop on Clichy. She has forgotten her keys but seems surprisingly calm about this.

"Hopefully Naomi will be there to let you in?" I say.

"Oh, she is." Emily raises her phone. "We track each other."

I exchange a look with Sandra and suppress the urge to launch into a monologue about the surveillance state. Emily is not, in fact, my daughter. Sandra has remained silent for most of the afternoon, presumably equal parts amused and anxious over the exchanges Emily and I have been having. She told me earlier that despite all the absurd language, she's come to feel protective of Emily.

Sandra takes us on a shortcut that skips the noisy Place de Clichy roundabout. It is less empty up here in the 18th. Fewer people have left from this part of the city. We cut through narrow side streets. Glancing down, Emily spots a wallet in the gutter, under a motorcycle. She picks it up. There is no money in it, but all the ID is still intact. It belongs to a woman in her thirties who lives not far from here. Its placement under the wheel of the scooter, so that you would have to be looking in a certain direction, from a certain angle, to see it, makes it seem unlikely it was dropped.

"The pickpocketing up here is terrible," says Sandra, matter-of-factly.

Emily sounds distraught. "What should we do? Should I keep it? Should I take it to the police? Should we try to call her?" Her eyes dart frantically. She seems overwhelmed by a sense of obligation to a stranger's well-being. There is never not someone to make Emily do something, I think. There is, at all times, everyone living on her phone—real or imagined—who demand in one way or another that she consider everything.

In New York, we'd just drop it in a mailbox, I tell her. Perhaps you can do that here? After much fretting, Emily opts to keep it, walking us through all the steps she will take to return it to the owner as if she is testifying on her own behalf. First she will return home and call the wallet's owner. Then perhaps she will go by the wallet owner's address and ring her doorbell, but she doesn't want to alarm this woman, so when she calls her maybe she will leave a message and ask if it's okay to come by and ring the bell. If she cannot reach the woman, she will go by the *gendarme* station and inquire. But she is also anxious not to leave the wallet with the *gendarme*, because they cannot always be trusted.

"It's hard to know what the right thing to do is," she says.

And just like that, all my generous theoretical sympathy goes sailing right out the window. I'm an hour into my time with Emily, and it turns out it is I who may not have enough emotional space for Emily. The fact I could probably tell her this and she would understand is maybe the most alien part of this entire afternoon.

I get on a Vélib' and say my goodbyes.

"You're a really nice person for taking care of this," I tell Emily, sincerely. "You *could* always just call her and tell her when she can come by and get it."

I tack on this last remark in case she needs permission to not go the extra mile here. Emily nods, clearly unconvinced. I resist the urge to say make up your own bloody mind and get on with it! Possibly I have learned something, because I recognize Emily probably does not currently have the emotional space for me.

"Oh," says Emily. "Okay, maybe I will do that."

I resist the impulse to ask her if she knows how to get home, and pedal away. For a while during lockdown, the fact I had no one keeping tabs on me felt, at times, like such a punishment that, even now, it takes me a moment to recognize it as a freedom.

Le Football

finally invite the twenty-seven-year-old South African professional
soccer player over. He has been messaging regularly for a few weeks.
"Just checking in," he will say. "Would love to see you."

"So many twenty-seven-year-olds," Ellie jokes.

By now, I know I can have what I want when I want it, and because
of this the feral frenzy of swiping has subsided. I have winnowed down
the conversations to those who can hold my attention.

I tell the soccer player he can come over that night if he wants. It's
a Wednesday and I have no other plans. He says he'll come to my flat
after finishing practice from north of the city and messages me along
the way that the trains are slow. But "I am coming!" he says.

I pour myself a glass of wine and put on a Nina Simone playlist.
The noise from the street gently filters in. This is the bone marrow of
life. The swirl of the stars. The solitude of the rooms. The voice of
Ms. Simone. The pleasure.

When he arrives, we sit and have wine together and he tells me about his training, about his injuries, about having to learn French after he was drafted. I'm enjoying the conversation.

Do I want him to stay? I'm aware I can easily send him away. I can tell him tonight will just be about kissing. That all I want is a massage. That actually I just prefer to sit here and talk. I linger over my wine deciding what I will do. When he finally moves to take my top off, I let him. He stops and regards me naked. "Don't take this the wrong way," he says. "But you are so much hotter than your photos." I laugh that anyone could take this the wrong way. Also, I like my photos. But I am finding what I'm relishing most about some of these encounters is the pleasure I take from observing others enjoying my body. No one has told me that in my midforties this kind of gratification would be such an easily accessible enjoyment. And my body *should* be enjoyed.

He walks me to the bedroom. This is a different sort of youthful energy. He knows what he wants. I wonder what sort of position he plays on the field. Not that it would mean much to me if he told me. My knowledge of soccer is basic even for a North American raised on baseball and hockey.

"Do you just want a massage?" he asks. "Or do you want more?"

"I want more," I say.

He removes the rest of my clothes for me.

"Do you want more?" he asks again a short while later, returning his head between my legs, adjusting my thighs. "I do," I say. "What do you want?" he asks more than once. "*Encore*," I say with a smile.

He likes the reflection in the mirror when he is standing. "This would make a good video," he says. Will we ever again understand pleasure as an experience that doesn't require an audience to be true? I wonder.

"No video," I say, just to be clear.

He laughs and changes position. He wonders if the bed is too high, but we try. "Tell me if it's too much." I appreciate his understanding of his responsibility over his attributes. He takes his time.

Afterward, he stays over, having missed the last train. Rather, I let him sleep over. I like the way he talks. The stories he tells of growing up on another continent. I try to remember the last time I shared a bed. We initially fall asleep with his arms wrapped around me, and it feels comfortable, the most intimate thing we've done. But then we shift. He sleeps more than me. In the movies sex workers always forbid kissing as if that is the trapdoor to heartbreak. But it seems to me the sleeping embrace is far more risky.

"There really is no such thing as casual sex," I say to the group the next day over drinks.

"Just because it's casual, doesn't mean it's meaningless," says Nina.

TWELVE

Time and Again

'm inside the Bois de Boulogne, by myself and without a phone signal.

Worse, it's midnight. Possibly after midnight. I don't know exactly because I've turned my phone off to conserve the small amount of battery I have left, so that if I do find a pocket where connection seems likely I can use it. There are very few lights in the park. Ahead of me the gravelly road forks and disappears into the darkness.

Amazingly, this is my first time inside the Bois, a sprawling park on the west side of Paris, just outside the Périph. As much as I love Parisian parks, I never come out here.

The Bois was once an actual forest (*bois*), a hunting ground for the wealthy. It has a storied history.

In *D.V.*, Diana Vreeland's slim, rollicking memoir, she recounts visiting the Bois in her childhood in the early 1900s and seeing the "cocottes"—the "women of the demimonde"—parading through the park in the morning hours in their glamorous dress.

> That was the secret of the beauty of the demimondaines. They took the morning air. . . . Then they went back home to rest, for a massage, and to arrange the menus of the evening for their gentlemen friends. . . . And what clothes I saw in the Bois! I realize now I saw the whole beginning of our century there. Everything was new. . . . There's never been such luxury since. These women *looked* rich.

In Colette's *Chéri*, Léa watches the women passing her window on the way to the Bois and notes that the "skirts are changing yet again . . . and hats are getting higher." She resolves to visit her dressmaker and update her wardrobe.

I came to know the *parc* through its reputation as a haven for sex work, despite many efforts on the part of Parisian officials to eradicate the trade from the *parc* grounds. The only other stories I seem to hear about the Bois are about people getting mugged while walking through its more remote parts.

I have no sense of the degree to which any of this is true, or whether these are narratives that were once very true and have simply been permanently attached to the name regardless of the current reality. If my Google Maps was accessible, I wouldn't worry about it at all, I'd just leave. But the Bois is quite large, two and a half times bigger than

Central Park. Unlike Central Park, I can't spot the tops of buildings to guide me out. It's just darkness.

I have other options. Behind me, down the road I've just come up, is a small lake and a dock. Every twenty minutes or so a small ferry arrives to take passengers across the dark water to an island with a bar, where there is a dance party happening. I was the only person to take it back, just now, and I could easily return. Nina, Aarti, Sandra, and Ellie are all back there on the island, dancing, taking selfies with charged phones that work, and have better connections. But I don't want to go back. I'm too out of step with the night.

The evening starts with great potential. We plan to meet at Ellie's for dinner before going dancing at a club on an island in the Bois. It's the sort of evening I'd spent longing for during those months alone. The sort of evening I'd imagine and then shop for in my closet or online, trying on a seemingly endless array of outfits in front of my mirror before finally returning to my couch in my usual sweats. Now, finally, an actual reason to dress up.

It's not lost on me that all the clothes I've brought with me—the many outfits, the many me's—have remained largely untouched, hanging on their slim velvet hangers on the wall, observing my comings and goings in the same red Monoprix dress. The same cotton tank. The same pair of jeans. It turns out the life I am currently leading is expressive enough that it doesn't need an outfit to help get me anywhere.

But tonight is calling for more.

I scan my selection. I pull out the vintage green jumpsuit that looks like the one Farrah Fawcett wore in a photo to promote *Charlie's Angels* when it first premiered. In the promotional spread, Farrah is standing with a silver gun, leaning against a pool table. Beside her lies a body of a young man in a tuxedo, a gun still held in his dead hand. The caption reads in part: *FARRAH, as Jill, reports unexpected shenanigans behind the eight ball. . . . No choir gown for this Charlie's Angel—she's ready for action in a soft and sexy lounging jumpsuit.*

I am also ready for action. I put on the green jumpsuit.

I meet Aarti and Nina at the Ledru-Rollin Métro and follow them down the steps. I know nothing about the Paris Métro. Less than nothing. Apart from using it to get from CDG to the flat, I've been on it perhaps four times; I always walk or bike. Nina walks me through how to buy tickets.

It takes us forty-five minutes to get to Ellie's (a thirty-five-minute bike ride according to my map). When we emerge, the light rain has stopped and the sky is glowing as though someone has held up a soft white screen to a bright light. If I hadn't been told I was in the suburbs, I wouldn't have known it. There is a *boulangerie* on the corner. Haussmann-looking buildings.

Ellie's place is a small one-bedroom. In French real estate speak, it's 2 *pièces*, thirty square meters. The metric system is a lost language for me; I grew up with it, but I've been in the States so long I now have to reach for it from where it is stored somewhere in the back of my brain. My niece and nephews in Canada scorn my inability to tell them the temperature in Celsius—"WHAT IS SEVENTY-FIVE DEGREES, AUNTIE GLYNNIS?? IF IT WERE SEVENTY-FIVE DEGREES, WE'D BE DEAD."

Ellie has laid out a table of food. A *planche* of sliced, cured meat, three types of cheese, one of which is now oozing onto the board. A small jar of jam. And a focaccia she has just pulled out of the oven. We add the bottles of rosé we picked up at the Monoprix before we boarded the train and the baguette I bought from the *boulangerie. Une tradition.* They are made to be eaten, not stored. The image of the Parisian walking and biking through the city with their baguette in hand or bike basket is one of those instances when clichés exist for a reason. When I visited Paris in 2015, not long after the terrorist attacks, I had coffee with a Parisian who recounted how, during the two-day search for the terrorists, they had all been confined to their apartments except to go out and get their baguette.

I wander to the window to look out. The light has shifted to its evening golden glow but still feels particularly bright. Even though it's still August, the temperature has started to cool.

I pull out my phone.

"Come to the window!" I tell everyone. "I have found the light."

Into Ellie's window we crowd as I hold out my phone.

"Oh yes!"

"Ellie, if I lived here I would only take photos standing in this spot at this time of day."

The practiced shuffling of women who instinctively know their best angle. Like old Hollywood pros who understand how to work the camera to their best advantage. Understand that it's not a reflection but a tool. We shift and turn and tilt and then shift again. And *voilà.* Here we are. A postcard for the good life. Five beauties in a window. Lipstick, hair, light. A classic of the genre.

It's in this spirit we leave the apartment an hour later. This time in an Uber. Squeezed in, masked up, windows open, we careen down the freeway and are dropped off . . . I don't know where, is the truth. I'm simply following. We're taking a ferry, I do know that, but I'm far more invested in finally being able to update my dating apps with these new photos to give it much more attention.

Which is one of the reasons I don't know how to get out of the park a few hours later. I have broken one of my cardinal rules, discarded from misuse more than anything: don't ever go anywhere you can't leave without help.

And yet here I am, lost in the dark in a forest.

The dance club we've come to on this island is up some flights of stairs from the dock. We can hear the beat of the music pounding into the air above us.

There are only a few people here, we quickly discover, perhaps because of the early hour. The portion of club we'd wanted to get to is closed off. Up near the bar there are rows of tables, under a canopy. There is a large family there celebrating something. Small children run around, their cries jarring notes against the boom boom of the club music. It's like a symphony trying to play at the same time as a DJ. We settle on some stools a few levels lower. Nina is wearing tight jeans and a tank. Aarti and Ellie are in short dresses and heels. Sandra is in vintage black lace.

There is a large group of young people near us. The women are in towering heels and Hervé Léger–like dresses that look like they came bonded to them. One of the men is dressed in head-to-toe purple pajamas. "Gucci," says Sandra with some disbelief. "I covered that show, but I've never seen anyone actually wear that out in the wild." She gives a small shake of her head. The men are sharply dressed. Taut and tall. One wears a football shirt. "I like the look of him," says Ellie. But they dance in a group with their backs to us.

Somewhere between the ferry and here I have become dislodged from the evening. The vision I had of myself when we left Ellie's flat is now the wrong vision. I'm not sure why, but I can't seem to fit it in anywhere. I've slid out of the rhythm of the night somehow. The night I'd been coveting all this time hasn't arrived. I'm the wrong me, or this is the wrong place. I'd been so high these weeks on connection, I'd forgotten the feeling of being out of place. This feels awful. Like I've inadvertently plummeted through some wormhole and am once again the awkward girl at the high school dance.

Ellie goes to get drinks, but I don't think I can drink my way out of this. There aren't enough people. Just the Hervé group and the five of us dancing in a circle with each other. Or four. I am sitting down.

Nina, Sandra, Aarti, and Ellie drink more and dance more, and I watch as the scene around them seems to dissolve from their view until they only know themselves and their energy and the circle of fun they have created. I am outside the circle. Every few songs I get up and try to join. Try not to be the person on the sidelines. But it's too far away from me.

Eventually, Sandra and Nina start making noises that they are getting too drunk and are going to leave. Yes, I say, I will leave with you. But then another song comes on, and more dancing and another drink, until it becomes clear I will sit here like this until 2:00 a.m. and navigate the intoxicated group home. Or I will leave and sort it out on my own.

I decide to leave and say so. No one is bothered by this. They are drunk and happy. "Text us!" they call, returning to the music. I'm a little irritated that no one thinks my trying to find my way home with no phone signal is a little worrisome. But the thing about expecting people to always let you do what you want is accepting they are not always going to do what you want. Also, I don't have to go. I could stick it out and we could all go together.

But I don't want to stay. I don't want to have a bad night. I don't want to not have fun. And I don't *have* to not have fun. So I leave.

And now how to get myself out of the forest.

It's shocking to understand how recent the notion of time travel is. Even more shocking to understand is how recent our notion of time itself is. On Instagram, I have bookmarked a video of Bette Davis being interviewed about the film *Hush . . . Hush, Sweet Charlotte*, in which she plays an aging Southern belle who is losing her mind. The host remarks how Davis has been making many appearances recently on live TV. "Taped television is just like live television," Davis responds, cigarette tilted assertively in her hand. She mentions a live event she had been at the week before, or was it a week? "When you travel by jet, you lose all sense of place and time."

At the time of the interview, 1964, the experience of losing all sense of space and time had not yet been given a name. Jet lag was not officially recognized until 1966, nearly a decade after commercial jet travel had been possible. Until then, it was a symptom without a diagnosis, a cheating of the clock. Prior to jet travel, one simply moved with the sun, making the adjustment to time zones so slowly as to be barely perceptible. I once sailed the *Queen Mary 2* for a travel story, and the experience of landing five times zones away feeling normal and fresh was revelatory.

Time zones did not exist until 1883. Our entire modern understanding of time is, in fact, largely the result of the railroads. Towns needed to coordinate their timepieces so that they could coordinate arrivals and departures. Capitalism put us all on the same clock. The construct of time, as we collectively now experience it, is not yet two hundred years old.

It wasn't until the turn of the century (the twentieth century, that is; prior to 1899 there is little evidence people marked a new century with any especial regard) that the concept of time travel arrived. In 1895, H. G. Wells, then just an aspiring writer, wrote the novel *The Time Machine* about a British scientist who invents a machine that allows him to travel through the fourth dimension. The novel was based on an 1888 short story with a similar plot, also by Wells, titled "The Chronic Argonauts."

It seems, up until Wells, no one had lost their sense of time and place to a degree that had led them to theorize what it actually might mean to be lifted out of one's timeline and placed into another. Apparently, before 1888 no one had fantasized about their regrets being rectified, or been consumed by the possibility of how they might redo their youth for a better outcome. No one had been swept away on an ocean of what-ifs, or if onlys. No one, it seems, had given much thought to how their fate might have been changed if only they were able to go back and kill baby Napoleon? (Baby Hitler didn't arrive until

1889.) Baby Genghis Kahn? Maybe meet Shakespeare? Or travel to the manger in Bethlehem? When Mark Twain fantasized about going back to King Arthur's court in his 1889 novel, the goal was to supplant Merlin and modernize Camelot. However, Twain's traveler can only go one way. Once in Camelot, he's unable to return and must make the best of it.

Our fascination with slipping the surly bonds of the space-time continuum seems to have arrived with the train and capitalism. And then went into overdrive after the Second World War with the arrival of the atomic bomb, hurtling into the realm of science fiction. After which, like Kurt Vonnegut's Billy Pilgrim, we all seemed to come unstuck in time in one way or another.

Or perhaps rather than "our fascination," I should say men's fascination. Women are never allowed to unstick themselves from time for some reason. Unless, like my mother in the late stages of dementia, who whirled round and round her own life as though caught in a centrifuge, we are betrayed by our bodies. Otherwise we are hooked to a physical ticktock from a fairly young age, never allowed to forget that we are being propelled forward, like it or not, in one direction. Instead of traveling time, we are required to battle it—or the appearance of it—with all our expendable income, never to enjoy it.

This should not, perhaps, come as a surprise: as with so much, the time travel storytellers were almost exclusively men (in Wells's *The Time Machine*, there is only one woman. Weena, a "little doll of a creature," described as "weak" and "futile" and while helpful to the cause, in the end left behind). As a rule, men don't seem very able to imagine a woman in motion separate from them. Children, yes, as we know from any number of classic children's stories. Women, no.

Out of the darkness ahead appears the Vélib' stand I was sure I'd seen on our way down. There is one Vélib' left. I cross my fingers it's a working one. I can't access the app on my phone to check. I type my code in. The stand beeps, the bike releases, I climb on and pedal up the hill to the fork in the road.

The time travel machine H. G. Wells conceived of was a bike. Or at least that's what the vague outline provided suggests. The writer James Gleick describes it as a "fantasticated bicycle." Wells was an avid cyclist. He belonged to a bicycle club, enjoyed flying around the countryside on two wheels, and may even have taken inspiration for his time machine from an early version of the stationary bike.

The Time Machine was published at the height of the bike craze in Paris. On my bookshelf at home is a framed poster, a gift from my friend Maddy, of a vintage advertisement for cycles and motorcycles. The illustration is the work of Jean de Paleologue, who went by the name Pal. It was originally printed in 1899, right before the century flipped, but the image was so popular it was reissued multiple times and redone by many artists. The illustration features a topless woman warrior standing alongside her bike. On one arm she wears a shield, gripping the bars of the bike with her hand. In the other hand is a downturned sword as tall as she is. From her spiked metal helmet sprouts long, sharp wings. Over her head, in large arching letters, is the word *Liberator.* The name of the company, presumably, but the message could not be clearer.

Bikes were revolutionary for women. They provided a way to get around that did not require a chaperone or permission (even sex workers, the only women allowed to walk the sidewalks alone, could only do so with a license from the city). They changed fashion for women. Goodbye to those long, tiresome skirts that might get caught in wheels. Hello to sportswear.

Naturally, there was a push to keep women off of bikes. One argument was that the placement of the seats might inadvertently cause unsuspecting virgins to experience an orgasm. Critics were not wrong to worry that women might experience a type of ecstasy on a bike. A friend who was doing research into the history of pornography for women once told me the reason women's pornography is rarely successful is because the thing women fantasize about most is freedom.

In *The Cost of Living*, Deborah Levy writes of her e-bike as though writing of a lover who helps her reinvent herself after leaving her marriage. Levy races up and down the black tarmac of a main road, imaging it to be an ocean, carrying her groceries up the hill to her home. It's not hard to envision her in a helmet with spikes and wings sprouting from it. She writes of a single middle-aged lady in her building named Jean who constantly harasses her to move her e-bike. She doesn't want Levy to let her bike stand, not behind a tree, not for two minutes. Levy wonders what needs calming in this woman. Did she feel "ashamed to be living alone, and was transmitting a portion of that shame" onto Levy? Had Jean "reluctantly stepped outside the societal story that offered her symbolic protection," and if so, "how was she to protect herself?" Reading that, I was left to wonder whether it was seeing Levy, so free and, in the moment, seeming joyous on her bike, so visible, that felt even more threatening to Jean? There is a certain comfort in invisibility, after all. Levy ponders: What was it Jean needed Levy to be, or not to be? Levy doesn't answer the question, but one assumes part of the answer is a woman less in charge of her own direction.

During the first lockdown I brought my bike upstairs to my apartment and parked it at the head of my bed. Stories abounded about deliverymen being attacked and robbed of their e-bikes in the city. Mine was not an e-bike, just a regular road bike, but the idea of leaving it out on the desolate New York streets felt akin to leaving a family member outside.

I don't have my helmet with me tonight in the Bois. Nor does the one I own have spikes. Nor am I topless (though there would be no one but me to enjoy it if I was). But the Vélib' makes me feel liberated from my uncertainty. At least I am moving.

One summer, the apartment I'm currently staying in was not available. Instead, I stayed for a short time up in Montmartre, in an airy treetop flat owned by an older woman who'd been there for a long time. Her preferred way of travel was on cargo ships. She told me there were a few spots open on each crossing that you could book. On her apartment walls were hung paintings of the sea she'd done on her many voyages. Montmartre is on a hill, on the north end of Paris. Until the nineteenth century, it was its own village. To get home at night, I'd often bike up Boulevard de la Villette, through the Belleville neighborhood, then across Boulevard de la Chapelle, alongside the elevated Métro tracks, beneath a series of stops: Jaurès, Stalingrad, La Chapelle, Barbès-Rochechouart. Stops I was familiar with only by reputation as the ones people I knew who lived in Paris avoided, or, when they did pass through, made special effort to keep their belongings to themselves. Whether or not the reputation was deserved, or like the Bois, ingrained from habit, I had no idea.

This was the summer that many refugees, having no other options, took up residence in camps under the tracks, no doubt allowed to remain as long as they did because the neighborhoods were considered, by those with power to make decisions, "less desirable" to begin with. Thousands of people—men, women, and children, fleeing or pushed—living in encampments in this narrow cement strip underneath the rumbling Métro. At night, when I pedaled by, they appeared to me as silhouettes; only sometimes would I glimpse an upturned face, or hear some notes of music. In the following months, the camps were repeatedly evicted by French authorities, and the people living there taken to "centers in Île-de-France" though I don't recall the locations of these centers ever being made clear.

I wonder, how must I have appeared, sailing by on a bike in the night? Free to come and go. Or even if I did appear. I, too, might just have been a shadowy silhouette.

Movement is only enjoyable when it's a choice. Bookended by places of respite and permanence.

The dark trees loom. There are no signs at the top of the hill. Or none that I can see. But there is a paved road, which is a good sign.

Suddenly a car appears from the left and continues by to the right. Are they entering or leaving the park? Is there some bypass through here for vehicles? There must be. We came here in a car, though I was so busy staring at photos of my own face that I don't recall from which direction. I turn to the left. *On y va.*

I stay on the paved road, assuming that at some point it will lead somewhere. There is no sense in panicking when you're alone. Particularly when your aloneness is the result of your own decision-making. Panic needs an audience to be useful. All I know is that at some point I will emerge from these woods, and when I do I will either get a signal and know where I am, or be able to see the rotating spotlight atop the Eiffel Tower and orient myself from there. Whether that spotlight revolves all night or not I actually have no idea. Maybe they turn it off at a certain hour. Though, again, I don't actually know the time, because I have no watch. In her piece about her packing list, Joan Didion says the one thing she always forgot to pack was a watch. She had everything else a person who prized control might need, but never knew what time it was. "This may be a parable," she wrote, "either of my life as a reporter during this period or of the period itself." Perhaps she was time traveling and didn't know it.

The trees don't appear to be letting up. I begin to wonder whether I have, in fact, cycled myself into the depths of the Bois, and if so, will I be here all night? And then, quite suddenly, I am spit out onto a thoroughfare, one of those points in Paris where a number of roads converge and shoot off from each other like a wagon wheel without a rim. I stop. I'm out of the woods, but I don't recognize a thing.

Paris can turn weirdly industrial without notice, and I seem to be in one of those areas now. All imagination and whimsy and grandeur have been wiped from the scope of living. As though, tired of all the beauty, someone came along and said, Let's try having none. French bureaucracy as architecture. There isn't enough traffic for me to make an educated guess which exit might be my bet. Actually, there is no traffic. A total of two cars have gone by. Based on very little evidence, I decide I must be inside the Périph and proceed, making sure to keep the trees to my back. If I am indeed on the other side—which I have never been on—it will probably be clear to me at some point.

I cross over the intersection and proceed down the widest anony-mous boulevard. Its four lanes are divided by a thick median of trees. After a few minutes, the buildings have resumed their traditional Haussmann appearance. It's all very grand and Parisian except I am the only person here.

Has anyone ever had Paris to themselves? Surely the answer must be yes, though it's difficult to imagine. It feels like the entire city has been laid out just for me. As I coast along, in my emerald green jump-suit, wide trouser legs flapping in the breeze, I try to envision other women whose paths I am unknowingly retracing. Women of the re-sistance. Women racing home to slip in after curfew. Women escap-ing. Foraging. Working. How many were simply enjoying? How will we ever know? It's so easy to feel as though you are the first at some-thing when no one has declared themselves as such before you. There are, as far as I know, no plaques commemorating women simply being free.

I hit another roundabout. This one is even larger. There *are* cars here. Not many, but more than I've seen all night. The intersection is truly enormous. Operatic. Without the direct reference of the park I have no sense of which way to choose. Or even what direction I'm facing. I might very well bike myself back to the Bois without mean-ing to. I'm not lost per se, just traveling without guideposts. Signage. Direction.

And then the great swoop of light.

I coast forward twenty feet and boom! There is the Eiffel Tower to my right. I have made good decisions. I sweep around the circle and soon find myself in front of the Trocadéro. I'm rarely over here, but I know it. I continue on, keeping the tower to my right and then behind me. There are no shortcuts in Paris, I remind myself. This almost never stops me from trying to make one, no matter that every time I do, I almost always find myself three arrondissements away from where I want to be. But not this time. I'm sticking with Parisian rules. I just keep going, and there, finally is the Seine. I'm by no means close to home, but at least it's a straight shot from here.

The dark water now beside me. The tall trees overhead. Both seem poetic and welcoming instead of threatening. The empty road. For twelve months I was allowed to be only one thing: a woman alone in the top-floor studio apartment. No matter how many outfits I con-structed for myself, that one truth remained.

It was especially jarring since for years I had been cycling through some variation of all the lives potentially available to me. Traveling back and forth through my own spliced timeline. Time spent as a caretaker to my mother. Time spent doing the school runs for my niece and nephews. Times spent being the resistor. The professional. The holi-day taker. The adventurer. The support system. The child carer. Then back to caretaker. Then back to soccer runs. Then back to travel. The envier. The envied. Sometimes I was all these people at once. The emo-tional jet lag of moving from one to the other often more intense than the real thing. No one, it seems, has ever successfully solved the problem of what happens if you meet yourself. But it felt to me that a lot of the time, I seemed to be in many places at the exact same time. This must be some other version of time travel. I am a woman with multiple lives, happening simultaneously in the same timeline. Modern womanhood, a time travel story.

Right now, I am the woman flying along the Seine in the green jumpsuit. The only moving figure against the backdrop of stationary, silent Paris.

THIRTEEN

Woman Reclining

feel, for the first time in a very long time, that I am in full control of myself.

I'm also vaguely aware that I have become the very thing we are taught to fear. A woman unafraid of her own desires, freed from the expectation of asking permission to satisfy them, even briefly. There's not a shred of shame.

Something has been unleashed in these last few weeks. Women in myths are forever condemning the world to chaos in their search for knowledge—the apple bitten, the box opened. But I know plenty. I am not here to learn. I am here to feel. Perhaps I have simply unleashed myself.

Over drinks with the girls one night, when I recount the evening with the twenty-seven-year-old South African soccer player, Sandra quietly says:

"They are only interested because they know you don't want to get married and are too old to have children."

She says this in a way that I understand is intended as a jolt of protective reality in this mildly hedonistic tour I have set myself on. She is trying to be a good friend. Over the years, Sandra has watched a fair share of Americans land here with American-in-Paris romantic dreams and then been tasked with dealing with the aftermath of those dreams eventually imploding in a divorce court system that heavily favors men, particularly when there are children involved. More than a few women in her life are painfully tethered to France until their child comes of age. She's worried I'm at risk of veering a bit too close to the cliff that will tip me into the French romance fantasy, and she wants to head me off before I take the plunge. But . . .

"Exactly!" I clap my hands together to emphasize. "This is precisely the entire point. I don't want those things either."

She looks skeptical, as though I am kidding myself. Which is entirely possible, I suppose. Who knows. Who knows how this is all supposed to go when it so rarely has gone this way in the past. How am I—well, forget me for a moment—how are *we* supposed to know we're in the right place if the destination is not a recognizable one? An aisle to walk down. A holiday to celebrate. I'm fortunate to have a life full of somewhat satisfied married friends, so the reality of married life, at least viewed up close, is not a blank slate for my fantasies. It's relieved me of the idea that marriage is a conclusion, or anything but another way to live. But without outside affirmation, I'm still left with the responsibility of having to trust that simply *feeling* enjoyment is evidence enough that where I am and what I'm doing is good and true and worthwhile.

.   .   .

On Tuesday I go to the Louvre. It's the third week of August, tradi-
tionally the emptiest week. Handwritten EN VACANCES signs are in
every door.

The last time I entered the Louvre was in 1994, during my three-
month backpacking trip across Europe when I was nineteen. It was
July. The French currency was still francs, and my only memory of
being inside the cavernous museum was that the *Mona Lisa* was much
smaller than I had imagined and that I could only view it from a distance through a cloud of tourists holding up VHS cameras. I have not
been back since.

No matter how empty the city has been in past Augusts, there has
always been a huge line snaking out of the Louvre entry. It's as though
the glass pyramid is some sort of magnet, pulling everyone in the city
with a foreign passport and return ticket home toward it. No thank
you. There are plenty of other museums in Paris.

This year, though, each time I Vélib' through the narrow, ancient
arc off Rivoli, and rumble along on the cobblestone to the exit that
will shoot me out along the Seine, I see no line. *No line.* I'm amazed
this emptiness still amazes me. But it does! The first time I notice, I
assume it's the day of the week the Louvre is closed. But then it happens again on a Friday. And again after that.

I buy a ticket.

The truth is, it's been so long that I have no real sense of what's
even *in* the Louvre. Is it a museum with a theme like the modern art
of the Orsay or the MoMA? Is it some of everything important like
the Met? I find large museums overwhelming. I try to limit my visits

215

to the Met to ninety minutes because after that I find my brain shuts off; I stop feeling fed by the art and begin to feel beaten down.

I decide to give myself the afternoon.

Normally when I'm in Paris, I aim to do at least one cultural thing a week. A museum or a gallery; there are very few live performances in August, though the summer before lockdown I saw a life-changing Patti Smith concert at the Olympia. The main story in the news that week was the burning down of the Amazon, and Smith did a blood-curdling cover of "Beds are Burning."

The Amazon might still be burning, I think, even if our awareness has been drowned out by everything else.

But I have done nothing remotely cultural this trip. I decide I will make up for it all with this visit.

I meet Aarti and Ellie up in Montmartre at our beloved brunch place beforehand. I arrive dripping in sweat from the ride up followed by all the stairs to Sacré Coeur. The chef—my crush—is not here. We sit in the back, near the windows, in the late summer light. This time I order the *chocolat chaud* and pour the warm foamy milk over the clump of chocolate at the bottom of the enormous round cup. I order the bur-rata cheese scramble, and we share *pain perdu*. I make Ellie pose in the light and take pictures until she is finally satisfied with one. The ones I find most beautiful, of her laughing, her head thrown back, she is unhappy with. She points to the curve of the jaw. The angle of the arm. She settles on a more contained one. Arms in lap. Precise angle. Half smile. We always want to exchange our aliveness for perfection.

Afterward, we part ways at the door. "Good luck at the Louvre," Aarti calls, as she heads to the Métro. No one can quite understand why I am spending my day like this. "It's all religious paintings."

Half an hour later I'm in the cavernous entry belowground. Light is streaming in through the high, pointed triangular glass panes of I. M. Pei's pyramid.

I'm not the only one here. People are scattered in small groups, unfolding maps, taking selfies in the light. I have no plan. There's nothing specific I want to see. Near the escalators that lead up to the next floor, I spot a photo of the *Mona Lisa* and an arrow. I follow that. I've never fully understood the appeal of the *Mona Lisa*, even as a child. I assume this is both a measure of my own lack of sophistication about art combined with what I suspect must be a normal response to anything that has been flattened by so many eyes over so many years. She's famous for being famous. Maybe if I stumbled upon her unaware I would think differently. And yet . . . I've seen the *Pietà* and been moved by its liquid marble beauty. The ceiling of the Sistine Chapel backed me into a corner for twice the time allotted and struck me dumb. I will never grow tired of *Starry Night*. Last October, when the MoMA finally opened its doors, I went with a friend and her daughter. While they took in Monet's lilies, I wandered away. The room where *Starry Night* is displayed was empty. I've seen *Starry Night* probably a hundred times, and yet I stood in front of it for a full ten minutes, basking alone in the singing stars as they danced around the canvas seemingly just for me.

217

I continue following the signs for the *Mona Lisa*, this woman of mystery renowned for being still and impenetrable and silent. Three things I hope never to be. Maybe I will discover something new.

In my memory's eye, she lives in a hallway, but these days she hangs at one end of a large square room with vaulted ceilings, facing Veronese's enormous *Wedding Feast at Cana*. Rope barriers mark the pathway to her, as though she is a customs agent or a bank teller. There are probably twenty to thirty people in line waiting to take a selfie with her. In the middle of August, in year two of a pandemic, the *Mona Lisa* can still draw a crowd. I join them. I catch a glimpse of her through shuffling heads and shoulders. She's bigger than I remember her. I last three minutes. I'm not spending my time in line for a painting that fails to do anything for me. The entire point of coming here was to *not* stand in line. I walk around the side, toward the doors to the next room. I pause and I take a sideways look at her from ten feet away and am suddenly reminded that it *is* extraordinary to see the real thing. Hello there, Mona Lisa. How we love a silent woman. And then I continue on my way.

I return to the main hallway. The Louvre is essentially two long prongs with a vast courtyard in the center. Once you enter the museum, you walk the perimeter of it, floor by floor, back and forth. I'm currently on the second floor (level 1, to the French) and stretching away before me is a grand hallway that reaches so far, the far end appears misty. I can spot only five or six people in the distance. Overhead, the arched gilded ceilings are covered in frescoes.

I walk along, the paintings soaring above me. Each piece of art feels enormous. They *are* enormous. And dark. And bloody. If Van Gogh's stars sing to me, these scream. In this silent museum, I begin to feel as though I am walking through an opera, navigating a world that only consists of the extremes of human passion and suffering. There is nothing between me and what is being experienced in each painting. No bodies to maneuver around, no shoulders to peer over, no noises to anchor me to my own time and place. No overheard comments. No guide. No filter whatsoever.

So much agony. Nude women collapsed at strained angles. Bodies stretched in grotesque shapes. Blood. Mortal wounds. Rage. Grief. Terror. So many angels. Angels in the architecture, spinning in infinity. Hallelujah. Paul Simon seems deeply anachronous to this tour, but the line lodges in my head, nonetheless. God in all his vengeance. The gods in all theirs. The frailty of skin.

Room after room appears before me like waves, increasingly intense. After the last two years, these images feel less remote. It's easier to recognize the suffering and uncertainty they depict as something we are connected to instead of belonging to a distant past. I do not encounter any joy. As I understand it anyway. There is certainly a lot of rapture.

I'm sure if I knew more, had studied more, I would note the differences, be aware of the small strokes, the subtle meaning each artist tried to convey in each piece. The references. But all together it feels like a chorus. The unforgiving gods. The glory and violence of war. Men.

All to myself.

It's a lot.

Without realizing it at first, I'm drawn to the women. My phone emerges as if by its own volition to capture them, sometimes isolating them from the rest of the painting. It's not until I go up to the next floor that the women are released from their torment at the hands of gods and men and begin to appear on their own. Clothed. Confronting the

219

viewer directly, as it were. Perhaps this was the original fascination with the *Mona Lisa*: direct eye contact. Absence of torment.

It's here I begin to find myself.

Tucked into a corner in one of the smaller rooms—I've lost any sense of where I am, the last security guard was three rooms ago and there doesn't seem to be anyone else on this floor—I come across a painting of a woman lying on a blue velvet bed, among blue tapestries. Her nightdress is raised up to expose her ample bare bottom, and thighs that most definitely do not have a gap. Her head is turned coquettishly over her shoulder, so she is looking directly back at the viewer. A smile playing on her face. It is an inviting look. A familiar look. She most definitely seems to be enjoying herself.

The name of the painting is *L'Odalisque* and the artist is François Boucher. According to the plaque it was painted in 1745.

The woman in the painting is thought to be his wife, Marie-Jeanne Buzeau. Marie-Jeanne was an artist in her own right. She painted miniatures of her husband's work and also did portraits and tapestries. Something about her expression suggests he opened the door and surprised her, but that the surprise is welcome. Perhaps she was waiting for him. Perhaps she had summoned him. She is not unhappy he is there. The spirit of the painting suggests that Boucher was trying to capture something of their relationship. That encountering his wife as such was a not unreliable part of their marriage.

There is something about the look in her eye, playful but commanding, that I recognize. It brings to mind my evening with Blindfold.

Not the mechanical pleasure of it; the entirely enjoyable, if not life-changing satisfaction achieved. Instead, the pleasure I have taken from the memory, a pleasure that increases instead of fading away, is what comes from the knowledge that I summoned what I wanted, and it came. It is the pleasure of power. Of being powerful, mind and body. And to have that power emerge while in a position, literally, of almost complete vulnerability.

The other thing I've been considering in the weeks since is how it's possible the only surprising element about that entire encounter is how *not* shocking it was. The vastness of the divide between the way what I had done would read or sound in the telling versus how mundane it was in the doing. The actual *petites morts* ended up being the least interesting and, as it turned out, least enjoyable parts.

A few years after completing this painting, Boucher would paint two other odalisques, both known as *L'Odalisque Blonde*. The subject of each is commonly assumed to be Marie-Louise O'Murphy, fourteen at the time, and newly engaged as King Louis XV's mistress, his youngest. It was a role she'd maintain for two years, until the imposing Madame de Pompadour, Louis XV's official chief mistress (widely considered to be the greatest mistress of all time; she was the tastemaker of her age, and owned and decorated the Palais de l'Élysée, which remains the official residence of the President of the French Republic), felt he was growing too attached to the young Marie-Louise and removed her from court in the middle of the night and promptly married her off to a member of the French upper class.

The dictionary defines the term *odalisque* as "a female slave or concubine in a harem, especially in that of the sultan of Turkey." The odalisque was a popular subject in European art throughout the nineteenth century. In the aftermath of the European colonization of North Africa and parts of the Middle East, these paintings depicting "exotic," scantily clad women—women in rooms created for male pleasure— were hugely popular. Eventually they became the main component of the artistic movement known as Orientalism, during which Western artists became preoccupied with representations of the East. Or their idea of the East. Over time, the term *odalisque* has become shorthand to refer to a reclining nude female figure.

Arguably, the most recognized odalisques are Matisse's, but they are not in the Louvre. Painted more than a century after Boucher's, Matisse's are a series of women reclining, primarily on their backs (no bare bottoms here). They are either nude or clothed in loose garments, painted against "exotic" Orientalist backgrounds. To my modern eye the women appear to be dressed in the sort of caftans that are the mainstay of my summer New York wardrobe. They appear to be the ladies who lunch, whose spacious decorated rooms and seemingly leisurely lifestyles I crave. In reality, they were anything but.

Matisse began his series after escaping Paris during the First World War and relocating to Nice, in the South of France. He had traveled to colonial North Africa before the war and been mesmerized by the colors and shapes and people. Living in dreary wartime, winter Nice and feeling nostalgic, Matisse attempted to recreate the brothels of North Africa in his studio. He worked with a model, former dancer Henriette Darricarrère, then aged twenty, having her pose for hours.

According to Matisse's biographer Hilary Spurling, Darricarrère was a full participant in this brothel-inspired setup. She would be his most frequent model in these paintings before turning to painting herself, eventually (and with Matisse's encouragement) successfully submitting an entry into the Salon des Indépendants in Paris.

I can't make myself move on from Boucher's *L'Odalisque.* In some ways I feel like I'm looking at myself. Not just the expression, but her entire mannerism. The way her body lies across her bed. On my phone are several photos of me in a similar pose that I've been exchanging with men in recent weeks. But even more than that it's in the richness and luxuriating both here and in Matisse's paintings that I find a fuller representation of the life I've been leading this month. I'm not sure how I am supposed to feel about that. I'm twice removed from the subjects I'm seeing myself in. The odalisques that, in Matisse's case, began with the women in the brothels of North Africa, to the French model appropriating them and their culture, to me. Three times re-moved, if you count the male gaze they must travel through to meet me.

I think of the women from whom these images originate. Nameless, faceless (to some degree), relegated by circumstances of time and place to lives devoted to male pleasure. To what do I owe these women, as I gaze on their images and see my current life. Anything? Does the source of the art restrict me from seeing other elements in it? Is it a triumph to be empowered by something that capitalized on disempowered women? Or the ultimate exploitation. Whose story is getting told?

When I published my first book, I ceased to have control over how people related to it or to me. Regardless of what the truth of my experience was. But their iterations were built off *my* original narrative. Is it enough to simply acknowledge there is an untold story here, and also, that I can take some pleasure in the one that is presented to me?

I think of the twenty-seven-year-old Italian with the flowing hair and beard who rerouted his trip to the airport to come and see me the other day. I think about our spontaneous afternoon together and how once the clothes were off, the calmer I got, the more anxious he seemed to become, as if a transfer was taking place.

I think about how, once all this late twenty-something energy was spent, he suddenly (and reasonably) became rather anxious about making his flight. The confidence he arrived with depleted. The awareness of what he'd done seemed to wash over him and carry him away. He struck me as suddenly uncertain of his own desires. I wonder, too, what he saw in the light of depleted passion. A line from the last pages of Colette's *Chéri* floats in. "Her chin double, her neck ravaged, she recklessly offered herself up to his unseen gaze." My neck is unquestionably the most ravaged part of my body, and not ravaged in any of the good ways so many men are currently professing the desire to carry out.

Or perhaps I represented a fantasy fulfilled, and sometimes fantasies are best left to be just that. In *Fear of Flying*, Erica Jong's heroine, Isadora Wing, finally lives out her "zipless fuck" on a train fantasy, only to find herself revolted instead of turned on. I imagine that by the time the Italian gets on his plane, or arrives on the other side, this encounter will begin its transition in his life from whatever has unnerved him—I'm doubtful it's my neck; I think more likely it can be unnerving to let your desire run the show—into what it will become: the story of the time he pursued and consummated with an older woman on a wild trip to Paris in his twenties. Will I emerge as a figure of mockery? Scorn? Perhaps at first, but not totally. I imagine I will eventually become evidence of his adventurous spirit. I see his belly growing, his hair—hung onto as evidence of a person capable of more—thinning and graying, as he settles into his life. I become, the more comfortable and predictable his life gets, a cocktail party tale. What I see as an act of summoning by me, rewritten by him as an exotic conquest.

And what does he become in my life? You find some version of him here in my tale. Likely just as removed from how he exists in his own world as I am from his. Filtered through my depiction, and my enjoyment, for my purposes.

In a 2015 essay, the Canadian writer Najwa Ali wrote that viewing odalisques demands that we look outside the frame and see the world through the prostitute's eyes. See their depiction in art as the artist's "fetish." A "sign of the flâneur's movement, his ability to enter a netherworld, his ability to move anywhere." And the prostitute as the woman who was moved. "Who opened her legs or had them opened for her."

I currently have the ability to move anywhere, a fact I have never been more aware of than this month. And I have the ability to command what I want to come to me; I can open my own legs, or direct someone to open them for me. Or just allow them to. Whatever I want. I seem to be, in the life I am currently living, both the flâneur and the odalisque.

I've been in the Louvre for at least an hour and haven't seen another person since I left the *Mona Lisa* to her adoring line. I understand, I'm hardly the first person to have the Louvre to themselves. What makes my solitary experience of the museum unusual is the time of day and the fact I am neither wealthy nor connected. People can and do pay to have after-hours tours, when the museum is closed to the public. The museum courts donors by allowing them to enjoy this privileged space without the masses. I'm just here.

In 2010 the photographer Nan Goldin was offered the opportunity to tour the Louvre alone after hours and photograph the art. "It's a rare artist who gets to wander barefoot through the Louvre during its off hours photographing anything she likes," wrote the *New York Times* of her venture. It's the detail about being barefoot that has lodged itself in my mind. As if she wanted to be as close as possible to what she was trying to connect with.

Goldin first launched herself into the art world with her show *The Ballad of Sexual Dependency*. She had spent years photographing her own life and the lives of those around her in early eighties Boston and New York: queer people, trans people, sex workers, gay men and women, herself perhaps most of all. A decade later many of her subjects would be gone, obliterated by the AIDS epidemic. Goldin is still here, though.

That late-night barefoot Louvre tour resulted in a show titled *Scopophilia* ("the love of looking," a term mainly applied to the sexualizing male gaze of Hollywood cinema); she paired photographs she'd taken of the Louvre masterpieces with her own archive. Eros and pain across the centuries. She included in the show a photograph of *L'Origine du monde* (*The Origin of the World*), Courbet's famous painting of the vulva, which must have been on loan to the Louvre at the time.

In *L'Origine du monde* almost all of the woman's body is outside the frame. Instead, the focal point is the vulva. The pubic hair. The upper part of the spread legs, the buttocks, the pinkish-hued folds of skin peeking out. In the upper corner, a glimpse of a nipple. The painting normally lives at the Orsay, where it was only put on permanent display in 1995 (Michelangelo's *David* was immediately placed in a public square upon its completion in 1504); Annie Ernaux wrote that she regretted no woman had ever produced a painting of the female genitalia as "indescribably moving as that by Courbet." One time I was at the Orsay and encountered a family of four standing in front of *L'Origine du monde*, the preteen son and daughter smirking uncomfortably, unsure of where to put their eyes.

Inevitably, Courbet's painting is criticized for its pornography. The woman reduced to a body part. We know nothing else about her. No face. No limbs. No clothes to tell us what her life might be outside the frame, or what she brings to this pose. Just the folds between her legs and the hint of a nipple. The extremity of the male gaze. The painting as a sort of glory hole.

I hadn't gone to the Orsay to visit it this trip, but *L'Origine du Monde* has been on my mind these last weeks as I've fired off similar-looking photos both to men I know nothing about, outside the frame of what they've provided in their profile, and some that I do. I think it's unlikely I will see the South African again in the time I have left, but that hasn't stopped us from exchanging images of ourselves that are unquestionably pornographic. I have reduced myself to a body part, which at the age of forty-six, the age I am reassured is when I can expect to slide out of every gaze and directly into invisibility, feels electrifying. If it is not true that I am made invisible by my age, what else might not be true? Perhaps none of it is true. Who could have guessed this would be the knowledge acquired by my taking a bite out of Fruitz.

As we begin the cultural archeology of digging into the lives of the women depicted in art—one upside to the internet's insatiable need for content—we are encouraged to interrogate our own gaze. How are we looking at these women? Who were they actually? What were the circumstances that led them into the frame, and what has been left out, either because the artist didn't care, or didn't know, or didn't want to know? All necessary thinking to give three-dimensionality to people relegated to a two-dimensional existence.

Najwa Ali writes of Matisse in North Africa: "There are massacres—somewhere outside the frame. Matisse complains only of weather. Paints flowers obsessively and sometimes Zohra [Zohra being one of Matisse's inspirations for the odalisque], the local girl, maid, prostitute, whatever. Zohra."

Whatever.

Women are the whatever, until they are the ones telling the story. But I sometimes wonder if by acknowledging only their exploitation we are not just flattening them in another way.

I wonder, for instance, at the woman who spread her legs for Courbet. How much of the decision to do so was her own? How much power was she exerting in that moment—on him, on the world? Any? None? A great deal? Perhaps she enjoyed it. Perhaps she wanted to be enjoyed without the punishment that inevitably comes when a woman reveals her face while asserting that erotic power. Perhaps this was the only kind of power she was able to assert. Or the culmination of her power. Perhaps this was the only way to tell her story. I have no idea because this was the only way she was able to be seen. The rest is left in silence.

Much like the *Mona Lisa*, the identity of the model in Courbet's painting remained a mystery until very recently. A few years ago, a male French historian identified her as Constance Queniaux. Queniaux made a successful living in the late nineteenth century as a dancer in the Paris Opera Ballet, as well as a courtesan (the French sometimes refer to this lifestyle as a woman devoting herself to a life of "galanterie," which was also an old British slang word for vagina). *L'Origine du monde* was commissioned by Queniaux's presumed lover, Khalil Bey, the Ottoman ambassador to France at the time. Bey reportedly kept the painting behind a green curtain, only revealing it to select visitors. A sort of sext meets my last vulva scenario. He eventually sold it to pay his debts. He was not the only man to do so. The painting's final owner, a French psychoanalyst, donated it to the state to pay off his taxes, continuing that long tradition of men finding financial security off images of women's bodies, which is how it came to the Orsay.

Queniaux, meanwhile, lived and died a wealthy woman. After leaving the world of *galanterie*, presumably with the money she made in it, she established herself as a well-respected philanthropist and managed, whether intentionally or not, to disengage her name from the famous painting.

My current gallant life seems unlikely to result in this sort of wealth. Though it also does not require me to bear the burden of revulsion either. Jackie Kennedy once remarked to New Yorker critic Judith Thurman that she was unsurprised many French courtesans ended up preferring the "Sapphic" company of women in the end: "the touch of those ghastly old toads who kept them would have sent anyone rushing into a woman's arms." I am always rushing into my female friends' arms, but for friendship, and not as an antidote to unwelcome if necessary touch.

I also know I am not in the position of having to disengage myself from my own actions. What would happen, for instance, if one of these *origin* photos I have taken of myself made their way into the world? There are plenty of people whose lives would still be—and are— derailed by this sort of revelation, and the shame that would follow. But would I? I'm a woman in her midforties, past cultural expecta- tions of appeal or potential, who makes a living off of self-revelation. I imagine I would take the opportunity to turn it into a story and get paid for it. Which is another sort of gallant life, I suppose. Owning your narrative, to the extent anyone can, is a sort of superpower rarely available to women. A woman freed from shame, a character too ter- rifying to contemplate for most storytellers.

This is not the first time I've seen my life reflected back to me in sex workers of the past. It often seems the only way I find myself in classic paintings, regardless of how much sex I'm having in real life. In 2015, I went to a large exhibition at the Orsay titled *Splendors and Miseries: Images of Prostitution, 1850–1910.* The artwork that impacted me the most in that show was a Van Gogh painting of a serious-looking woman at a Montmartre café having a drink alone. I'd been traveling alone for weeks at that point, and though of course the dress was different, I saw myself in that woman, enjoying her solitude at a café table in Paris. I had been doing just that, that very morning. The label to the right told a different story, of course. The only woman who would have been allowed out in the world without a chaperone, let alone to have an alcoholic drink, would have been a prostitute.

For a while now, my computer desktop photo has been a Suzanne Valadon painting titled *The Blue Room.* It's a self-portrait Valadon completed when she was in her midfifties. The painting shows a woman, heavy-ish set, with the ample bosom that comes with middle age. Thick arms. Dark hair. Cigarette dangling from her mouth. She is wearing a pink camisole, absent of any lace, and striped men's pajama trousers. The string around the waist visible in the folds of her belly. Her gaze is both direct and away from the viewer. She looks toward the end of the bed. As though she has been roused by someone coming through the bedroom door to find her reclining. She is making no apologies. If this painting was dated 2023 instead of 1923, it would not look out of place. Except perhaps for the cigarette, this is a portrait of the modern woman. I have dressed for bed like this since I was twelve.

The trousers she is wearing in the portrait were still somewhat radical in Valadon's time. While they'd appeared on a number of high fashion runways by 1923, including, of course, on Chanel's, this was still nearly a decade before Katharine Hepburn insisted on them. ("Do you ever wear a skirt?," Barbara Walters asked Hepburn during a 1981 interview. "I'll wear it to your funeral," came the gravelly response.)

Valadon was born in 1865 in Montmartre to an unwed single mother. Like basically every female model we encounter in museum paintings, she was raised in poverty. She began as a dancer before becoming a muse to a number of high-profile artists, including Renoir and Toulouse-Lautrec. She started painting full time in her thirties, eventually becoming the first woman admitted to the Société Nationale des Beaux-Arts. When she was forty-four she began an affair with the twenty-three-year-old friend of her son's who'd been her male model for a number of years and featured in some of her most controversial paintings. They married the next year and remained married for two decades. At the height of her success, she achieved enough financial stability that by one account she threw a new fur coat on the floor for her dogs to sleep on.

Valadon appropriated the image of the reclining woman in many of her paintings but shifted the view. In *Catherine Reclining Nude on a Leopard Skin*, a blonde woman is depicted doing just that (my lockdown habit of lying naked on fur was not an original one, it turns out). We see her from the end of the bed, the feet nearest to the viewer, the head at the farthest end, atop waves of a nude body. Valadon was never interested in propagating the idea of the ideal female nude. Even the breasts are in repose, slid back and to the side. The angle of the arms, the head fallen to the side, tells us this woman is actually asleep. Not posing, not performing rest. She is at actual rest. And yet, nothing about the painting suggests we are voyeurs in her abandon; she is comfortable in it whether we are present or not.

The alternate title of the piece was *L'Endormie*. The sleeping one.

I move through the rest of the Louvre allowing it to wash over me and carry me through. Somewhere between the two odalisques—the woman with the bare bottom, and the woman at complete rest—is where I am currently living. Between Boucher and Valadon. Between invitation and unapologetic abandon.

FOURTEEN

To the Sea

The five of us—Nina, Sandra, Aarti, Ellie, and I—are traveling to an island off the west coast of France, where we'll stay for seven days. To get there we've taken a TGV express train from Paris, switched to the local at Nantes, and are now waiting to board a ferry that's big enough to hold two hundred people. When it docks, it appears to be at capacity. We stand at the entry gate watching a seemingly endless stream of passengers disgorge in the afternoon light, carrying their bags, and their boards, and their rolled-up beach tents. Sun hats tied tightly on. Faces still rosy from the sun and salt. On and on they come while we stand alone at the gate waiting.

Finally, after what seems an eternity, we're allowed to board. There's no one going in our direction, it's just the five of us, plus three older men who are clearly locals. They have no bags. Just themselves, and rough clothes and weathered faces. It's the last few days of August.

Les vacances are ending and the French are returning to their city homes. We are doing the opposite. We sit on the top deck, letting the wind carry our hair and our dresses. Nina and Aarti snap group photo after group photo . . . *we must document!*

Before we left the mainland we went shopping for the necessary basics. The island has limited supplies, and everything will cost more. I let the others decide what is necessary and search out my yogurt and muesli and chocolate. Nina has had us all download an app that allows us to enter what we've spent so that at the end of the trip each of us will know what we owe or are owed, down to the penny. This alleviates the need for rounding up or down or good faith, or resentment when that good faith is not fulfilled.

Once we reach open water, the ferry slides up and then rolls gently down. I listen as the group plans out the week as if it's a math problem. On this day this, and on this day that. I will do this, I will do that. The phrase "It's a Build-A-Bear holiday" gets repeated over and over. I ask what a "Build-A-Bear" is and am told it's a toy store that lets you literally build a stuffed bear to your own specifications. I recognize what's actually happening is a setting of boundaries. A here's what I want and don't, here's what I must have and what I can do without, but without anyone having to say that explicitly. We are five women accustomed to having almost exclusive control over our spaces and our free time. This is a gentle attempt to draw personal maps of our week ahead to avoid transgressions, inadvertent crossings into valued territory that could lead to conflict. At the same time, I get the sense we're also trying to overcome a persistent, lifelong aversion to disagreement that even now, in these don't-give-a-fuck years, feels deeply difficult to break from. It's easier just to say, "Here's what I'd like," and then reinforce it with the declaration that everyone should do what they want. Even among the sharp elbowing of these individual declarations, I know they are not the sort of thing that gets committed to memory. They are the labor pains of delivering us into a new, temporary way of being together that will, in our future tales of the week, barely merit a mention, if they are recalled at all.

After a while, Ellie goes and stands near the ferry railing to get a better look at—and perhaps a shot of herself against—the open sea. We are sailing through shafts of light that fall easily on us. A gust of wind catches the short skirt of her dress, lifting it briefly and flashing her red lacy underwear. There are sounds of approval from the handful of local men who are up here, but they are good-natured. Instead, it is us who catcall aggressively, laughing wildly. Ellie remains where she is, tilting her head over her shoulder. Pretending embarrassment, though clearly thrilled. I tease her when she returns that her bra must also be red lace; she had told me she likes to match. "I like to always leave the house prepared for things to take a turn toward enjoyment."

The ferry ride is an hour. When we lose sight of the land behind us and begin to see the shadow of the island ahead, a pod of dolphins emerges. Tiny darts leaping out of the water in formation. Their black glistening bodies. The explosion of joy over and over. The sight of them must not be normal, or else there are so few of us on the ferry that concern over schedules has evaporated, because the ferry is turning. The engines revving up, the waves slapping the side of the boat, and we are circling them to get a better look. The old locals shout, "Dauphin!" and even their phones emerge. Up these gorgeous creatures leap as one, and back down, and up again. A tap-tapping reminder of how much life there is living around us. Eventually the ferry straightens out. The island reappears again in front of us. The only person not pleased by our unscheduled assignation is Aarti, who worries the boat's noise and movements are causing the dolphins harm. That what we see as joy is terror and the desire to escape.

And finally, the island. At the dock the line to board snakes down a long gangplank, along the quay and all the way back to the main street of shops. We disembark against all these French eyes, offering ourselves up for inspection.

"I hope my skirt doesn't flap up!" says Ellie, unconvincingly, as we descend.

We have all agreed not to location tag where we are. The island is popular with the French but not exactly well-known, so the tourists have not found it yet. There are no tourists this year to worry about, of course, but here, away from the city, in the open air, it is easier to slide away from the restrictions that have pinned us all down to a certain time and place and imagine the hordes that might appear once the clocks properly start again.

There are no cars allowed on the island. That is, no visiting cars, just the ones belonging to locals. Everyone bikes. We have all made individual reservations for a weeklong bike rental from the same place. It's only a five-minute walk from the ferry, and we trudge up, taking in all the storefronts, deciding which we think we might revisit this week.

The two young, lithe, dark-haired men at the bike rental speak very little English. Once we all pile in and Ellie explains who we are, they begin to roll out bike options. Some have baskets in front and only three speeds. Some have baskets in the back and ten speeds. Sandra has brought Marcel, so she has reserved a little covered cart for him that can be attached to the back of her bike. Ellie and I are the experienced cyclists; the others have varying degrees of confidence. They are going back and forth, weighing their options. There is some confusion over which bike offers what, and one by one we turn to Ellie for clarification, to articulate our needs, to declare our choices, this not that! To ask which she thinks is best. At each turn, Ellie keeps saying everyone can do what they want, even though in this instance it's clear that everyone needs help making a decision. Or help speaking French. Ellie and Nina have planned this entire holiday, down to the train and bike reservations. At some point, it must be their holiday too, and I can tell from Ellie's tone we are fast approaching that point. How easy it is to get lazy when there is someone else better at the work. Surely all of us could bungle our way through French bicycle rentals were we on our own.

Finally, we make our choices.

Nina's friend Nicolas is also on the island. He works a jewelry stand here in the summer and has borrowed a little car. He's come to pick up Marcel and our luggage and drive them to the house. We're responsible for pedaling ourselves there. After he pulls away, we set off, Nina in front since she is the only one who knows where the house we rented is located—the signal out here on the island is sketchy—and the rest of us staggered behind her. I'm reminded of the scene in *E.T.* when the group, E.T. bundled in a basket, races up and down the streets of California eighties suburbia to escape the authorities, finally lifting off into the air. The perfect encapsulation of the freedom afforded to children on two wheels. We all stagger along the rough roads. Our own encapsulation.

. . .

The sun rises at 7:26 here. Even though the night has been punctuated with sounds of doors being slammed shut by the night breezes that come through our open windows, I sleep in the cool island air better than I've slept in months. When I wake it's still dark. I'm unable to find coffee cups and end up using a paper cup for my Nespresso. Coffee by any means necessary.

I go to the garden, where there is a long wooden table and some chairs. Behind me birds flap their enormous wings in the trees. To the right a dove still coos.

Then the bells begin.

It's 8:00 a.m. Monday.

I count along with them. I like the poetry of this shared time. The church with the belfry is down the road in the nearest village, a ten-minute walk away. I sit with the birds and the flowers, imagining everyone following the same count. Measuring their days, however different they may look, by the same ring.

After eight rings, there is silence. I return to the birds and the shifting light in the garden as the sun rises high enough to set the fuchsia flowers on fire.

And then the bells begin again. An army of bells. A cacophony. A stampede. On and on they go. I unconsciously begin to count along with them again. And still they go on. Is it a holiday? Is there an emergency? Are people being called to the town square? Is this second round some sort of snooze button situation? Am I imagining all these bells? No one has yet emerged from our house with whom I can exchange a glance and an *Are you hearing this too?*

And still they ring.

Eventually, they peter out. Fainter and fainter. As if whoever is ringing them has just let them finish on their own, which is entirely possible, I suppose.

My count is 134.

I try to parse out the significance of 134. Is it the number of days of the year so far? The number of days left? Is today a local holiday on which 134 people died?

As I'm pondering this, one of the doors inside once again slams shut. Aarti's shutters, which face directly out onto this back garden, fly open.

"It sounds like cannonballs going off!"

"It's the price we pay for an airy house," I say.

In the kitchen, Aarti and Nina try to locate the coffee cups. It turns out they are in the large cupboards by the door I'd assumed was a closet, but in fact holds all the dishes. At around eleven, or when Ellie gets back from her run, we have second breakfast. So named by me after the hobbits who, in *The Lord of the Rings*, were devoted to their second breakfast. "Eleventy-one," my mother used to say to me when I was young. It was eleventy-one in the morning, or that was my age, or that was our departure time.

Here is our daily routine. To each, a duty. Nina scrambles the rich eggs with butter and cream. Ellie or Aarti slices the fruit, the avocado. Sandra or I sets the table. Each day we bring out everything that is currently open in the fridge. The hummus. The cheese. All the butter—we have three pounds and two different kinds, one with salt crystals and one with larger salt crystals that crunch in your teeth. To this is added the *baguette aux céréales* I purchase at the *boulangerie* each morning.

The *boulangerie* is in the village. After the bells I wander through the quiet lanes, amidst the thick shrubs, and past the low windows of houses painted various shades of pastel, until I pop out beside the grocery market and across from the *boulangerie*, which we learn the hard way on our first day closes at 2:00 p.m. In addition to the *baguette aux céréales*, I sometimes also buy *chausson aux pommes*, still warm from the oven. Or stop by the grocery market and replenish our eggs, as we go through a carton of eggs a day. And toilet paper, or coffee, and while I'm there, maybe a container of burrata.

Also on the second breakfast table is the large container of homemade kimchi Sandra brought from Ace Market on Sainte-Anne, which we add as a side to the eggs. More coffee. Bottles of bubbly water. Some chocolate.

Afterward, those of us who set up then clear the table, and everything but the frying pan goes into the dishwasher. The frying pan is placed in the sink to soak.

Then we scatter. To bikes, to beaches, to books, to midmorning naps. It takes resolve to scatter. But we practice.

In town one night we eat mountains of mussels, deep bowls of creamy sauce. We come early to secure a seat. The restaurant is on a side street in the harbor, back one from the main street. Even though there are few tourists on the island we still need to arrive when they open at 5:00 p.m. to be first, or else a line forms and we won't get a seat. The tables resemble card tables, and as we stand a little way away, waiting for the hour to strike, we watch the young women set them up in the street and then bring out the plastic folding chairs. We are second in line.

Ellie has *moules au Roquefort*, Nina has garlic, and Aarti and I both have the *grand-mère*, which comes with chunks of ham. Huge bowls stacked high with glistening shells. And baskets of bread and butter. Around us people come and go. Nicolas has joined us. He says Parisians from the 16th and 7th and 14th come here. From Versailles, they come.

"I see them and know immediately what part of Paris they live," says Nicolas. Some come from Belgium too. Because the king of Belgium has a house here.

"He is good," says Nicolas, "keeps to himself, doesn't make a fuss."

Afterward, I order the Nutella crepe I've been craving since spotting one in the train station the morning we left. It arrives enormous and thick with the chocolate-hazelnut spread. Just as we pay, the rain starts and becomes an island downpour. We slide under the narrow awning waiting for it to dissipate. It is heavy and then light, the way island rains are. Like waves from the sky emerging. Once it grows to a mist we dash for our bikes, which are locked up in rows by the harbor. To one direction, the sky is fiery red, with great shafts of gold shooting through. But to our left, and coming our way, it is black. We pedal quickly as though being chased, not out of fear of getting wet, but because the roads are not lit and our bike lights seem feeble against the wet darkness.

But the cloud stays behind us. I call to Ellie, as we slip off the main road, that I love when the sky looks like the sea. What is it about riding through the country at night. Riding anywhere at night. The satisfaction. The knowledge of a life well lived.

I'm prepared for the bells this morning. I count 186. Is this how many people were lost in the Second World War perhaps? A daily remembrance of casualties? The island was occupied during the war. This house has been with the same family for a long time. Perhaps since it was built. In one of the rooms is a deep closet filled with books dating back to the first decades of the twentieth century. The past seems very recent here. The bells stop. A rooster crows and the birds flap overhead, and the sky turns blue and gold.

We each settle on our favorite beach; like astrological signs, they represent some part of our personality. None are more than a twenty-minute bike ride from the house; some face the open water while others face the channel. The tides are dramatic on the channel side. At high tide there is a thin strip of beach, and at low it goes on and on, sometimes beaching the small craft anchored offshore. When the sea comes in, it can rise from your knees to over your head in a matter of minutes.

My beach of choice happens to be closest to the house, a downhill ride of three turns, and long stretches of road. It's called Plage des Sapins, the beach of pines, because between the beach and the road stands a thick strip of pine trees. Their tall, straight trunks remind me of the Black Hills of South Dakota. But here, the smell of pine mixes with the smell of sea. When I first come upon it after swooping around a curve, I feel as though I've slipped into something not quite real, as though this small forest may disappear in the night and not reappear for one hundred years.

I've brought with me *Wind, Sand and Stars,* Antoine Saint-Exupéry's memoir of being a pilot. Has anyone ever faulted a man for writing a memoir, I wonder. I'm in the second chapter where he writes about the wealth of comradeship. "Happiness! It is useless to seek it elsewhere than in this warmth of human relations."

I am always wary of advice given by men who've spent most of their lives doing what they please, and then, when it suits them, discover the joys of family or comradery. What else is there, they say, age fifty, wealth and success behind them. This marriage and fatherhood business is great! What else, indeed. We hear it as affirmation that the lives women have been living are in fact the correct ones, and not as an argument that perhaps they only feel like the ultimate choice once every other avenue of experience has been exhausted. A type of exhaustion women rarely know.

And yet. This island sojourn together *is* happiness. When our group shifts together it sings. In the evenings we lie on the couches, sit on the striped red chairs, sprawl across the floor, and read. So silent together that when I return from outside I wonder if the house is empty.

The bells begin. I count 181 this time, but perhaps I lost track. The others complain about "the fucking bells" but I love them. I love the

communal rhythm they bring to the day. I love that we're all hearing the same thing at the same time.

The pools in New York closed during the pandemic. It was the lon-
gest I'd been out of the pool since my mother registered me for swim
lessons as an infant. I spent those first summer months of lockdown
dreaming of water. Coveting cool immersion. Remembering the sensation of cutting through liquid, weightless. It is the only place, other
than my bike, where I feel completely at one with my body. Last summer, during an especially hot July week, I walked over to the foun-
tains outside the Met and sat there, dragging my hand back and forth
through the shallow icy water, weaving through it as though my hand
were a fish tail, before sinking my arm in as far as it could go.

Even though, in the grand scheme of things, my time away from
the water was short-lived, I still can't get enough of it. I bike over to
Plage des Sapins every day even if we make plans to go to another
beach later on. One afternoon, I go in the water as the tide starts to
rise. There are only a handful of others out here with me, including
an older couple who swims together. He is square and rotund; she
graceful and slender. The round transparent jellies, which we keep
trying and failing to identify via Google, float by. They are not the
stinging jellyfish is all we can sort out.

The tide comes in and the bottom sinks away. The rocky beach has
disappeared into the water and now is just ridges below, rising and
falling like the back of a serpent, out of reach of my treading toes. I

swim out to the little boat with the skull and crossbones flag. The boat call sign is Ye and a number. Apparently, all the island boats are Ye. I start saying we are luckye every time we encounter something beautiful.

Much later, Nina and Aarti arrive and find me reading in the trees. There is thunder rolling in, though no clouds to match it. In the interim the tide has gone back out. It feels like a dramatic costume change. I go with them for a swim, back down the now enormous beach, the ridges of stones hurting my feet. In the water we plunge, like the dolphins, over and over. When we emerge, we see lightning bolts far off in the sky. Nina counts the seconds. Can you get struck by lightning in water at this distance? Can you get electrified in the ocean? It seems unlikely. The water is too vast. And yet?

"If we do, maybe we will become superheroes," I say. "This will be our origin story. Holiday swimming off an empty island."

What will our superpowers be?

Nina says she wants the ability to teleport. She is tired of flying economy. Between her trips to Los Angeles to cover awards season, and the fact her boyfriend is moving back to the States at the end of the summer, the ability to teleport would be ideal.

"But if teleportation is not possible, then I'd like my superpower to be business class."

I say my superpower will be a high floor, north facing, pre-war apartment, with a low maintenance fee.

The lightning comes closer and we get out. Back across that long stretch to Aarti who is already in the trees. There, we wait for the lightning to pass before biking home along the wet roads.

.   .   .

The bells begin. I count 186 again. Well that's consistent, at least.

A light rain starts. I look up. The half rainbow that briefly emerged with the sun has become a vibrant full one. I adjust the umbrella on the long wooden table in the garden so I can remain sitting here, in the gentle sea rain, in the green and pink backyard, behind the white and green house, on a small French island in the Atlantic.

One evening I swim alone. The others have gone for a small plane ride around the island, but I've stayed behind. My desire to be alone outweighs the knowledge that I will likely later regret missing the ride. I eat carrots and hummus in the back garden and have a glass of white wine and then pedal back to the *plage*. In the water I take off my bathing suit entirely. Let myself "flap," as Ellie would say. I swim out far enough so that I can't touch the bottom and allow myself to float. Be carried. I'm in the water, halfway back to shore, my bathing suit in my hand, when the small plane passes overhead. I jump and wave and yell but I have no idea if my friends see me.

I forget to count the bells this morning. But Ellie has taken it upon herself to discover their significance. What do they mean? We must know the intention of these bells that inflict themselves upon us each day. "I'm going to call the tourist board!" Ellie declares.

.   .   .

We try a new beach today, this one at the tip of the island. Ellie's fa-vorite. Nina has stayed back for some alone time, which she is sud-denly frantic for. I think my taking it the other night opened the door. Nina has a hard time not being a tour guide, she tells me. She's going to clean. I tell her there is no tax for staying alone, you can just stay. She wants to clean, she says, and then . . . thank you.

This new beach is pristine. The sort that features on advertisements. Long smooth sand. Calm blue waters. Aarti is not a strong swimmer, having never learned as a child. How does one learn to swim as an adult, I wonder. Swimming works against every natural survival in-stinct you develop as an adult. It requires so much trust.

I'm a strong swimmer. I had lessons my whole life, and then years of competitive swimming, which I had some success at. In every pool I swim, my stroke is remarked upon, my sharp flip turns marveled at. Lifeguards move their chairs back to avoid the cascade of water I send their way. But how does one teach that to an adult brain? To be still. To have faith.

Still, I try to teach Aarti to float. "It's a matter of trusting the water," I say. "It will hold you if you let it." I tell her to lean back against me. I'm topless, my suit stripped down to my waist, and we joke about my bare breasts against her back. We have been here long enough that we're all familiar with each other's bodies. We have our inside jokes and routines: Sandra's After Eight mints, the five bikes in

the front garden, and all our talk of bodily functions. A new nonsensi-
cal language specific to this trip has developed—"Yann, and *obviously*";
"French 75 with prosecco"; "The water is cold, what did you expect"—
which will cease to have meaning the further away we get from this
island and these conversations, until everything becomes a feeling
rather than an account. Aarti manages to float on her own for at least
a minute, maybe more. "Goodye!" we say, clapping. "Well done ye!"

After, in the shade of a boulder, we watch six boys, age seventeen it
looks like, stand in a line and rub suntan lotion on each other's backs
with no discomfort. Then they get in a rowboat and go in circles, finally figuring out how to get as far out as the skull and crossbones.

No one can tell us about the bells. If 186 has significance it is unknown except perhaps to the individual in charge of the bells. The
woman at the church Ellie stops at seems puzzled that we would even
question their presence. There is no story behind the bells. They just
ring.

Today is my last day of being forty-six. Tomorrow I will turn forty-
seven and be a person in her late forties.

I get up early and go for a bike ride by myself to the rough west
coast of the island, which drops away in cliffs to the water. I lock my
bike in a gravel pocket and walk along a footpath that follows the

coastline. I pass an older woman walking her wiener dog, or maybe beagle, on a long leash. The leash trails behind the dog in the underbrush. French dogs, I have found, are similar to the French people in their formal disregard. In New York, dogs greet me with a smile. Here, even the friendliest dogs turn away from my open face. I once stood next to a young, energetic black Labrador on a sidewalk watching a marching band play "Rasputin" outside the closed Lux, and when I reached down to stroke his ears, he ducked away and shifted his head as though embarrassed by my actions.

Here on the cliffside walk, it is only us, yet the woman and the dog pass me by as though I might not be here.

Ahead, the waving grass. Beyond, the rough cliffs, the white-capped waves. Always the Atlantic for me. I'm reminded of the opening to *Portrait of a Lady on Fire*. The protagonist, a painter who doesn't hesitate to leap into choppy open water to retrieve her canvas when it falls in. Afterward she sits naked by a fire, smoking a cigarette. And then, later in the film, joins a wild witchy dance on the Bretagne cliffs before helping with a group-managed abortion.

With birthdays come assessments. I sometimes have to work to understand my life not as one long missed opportunity. The writing career not entered into earlier, when pay rates could actually support a life. The self-knowledge, so long in coming. The sex not had. The love not given or taken. But not today.

I see a cove and, when I turn a corner, come upon roughly cut steps that lead down. I descend, watching the sky and approaching dark clouds. I take my sandals off and sit on the rough sand and watch a sailboat out on the water. Going around the island? Down the coast? To Spain?

Yesterday, my friend Rachel sent me a decade-old video of us leaving our lower Broadway office when we ran a networking company there together. It's only forty-three seconds long and in it we are singing along to "Working Girl"—our office was on a high floor in the same building Melanie Griffith's character works in—as we navigate passersby on our way to the train. I watch it again and again and stare at my own beauty, which leaps off the screen at me, delayed ten years. My jawline. My eyes. My hair. I find myself coveting myself. And then I remind myself, I will covet this self too. This trip. This freedom. This joy. This movement and this skin I have now, even if parts are less vibrant than they were, they are more so now than they will be.

I know, too, that what the person in that video did not have was a sense of self. A belief in herself. A seriousness in life. Do I have it now? Do we ever fully have it?

I sit in the cove with the water and the sky on this island in the Atlantic and I think about my current photos and how my life would and would not appear to others were I to capture and push this moment out to the world. What would it invite others to think? And then I think, But what do *I* think about myself? That is the key question. The missing link this past year when I became a silhouette to myself. I don't quite know how to answer it yet—I have been successful in my determination to only feel this month, and not to think—but it seems the most important thing to be able to answer.

Perhaps there are not 186 bells on Saturday.

There are.

．　．　．

I go for a sunrise swim on my birthday. Biking along the empty hedge-hemmed roads in the deep blue predawn silence, down down down to the trees. The tide is halfway out and I walk the long beach in the nude, entering my new year the same way I entered my first: naked. The morning wind against my skin is making me aware of my entire body. I briefly wonder if this is something I could get fined for. We are not in the South; Northern France has different mores. But there is no one here. Me and the birds. Into the water I go, plunging down into the cold, that one brief moment between leaping and being submerged, suspended in the knowledge that you cannot stop whatever is coming. And then the shock of the cold and the gift of being fully and completely alive. I go farther out, leaping and diving until I can no longer touch the bottom, and then I lie back and allow the ocean to carry me into the next year. Forty-seven. Some part of me hopes to be seen out here by someone on the beach, if only to be carried away in their minds as a small example of possibility.

For dinner, we have huge plates of oysters and bottles of rosé. Ellie makes a *bûche au chocolat* and holds it aloft while everyone sings happy birthday in French, before presenting it to me like an offering. I'm still wearing the red Monoprix dress.

We race away from dinner. Literally. Nicolas's band is playing at a BMX festival on the other side of the island and Nina is anxious, after all he's done for us to secure this trip, that we are not late.

We form up our bikes and set off, Ellie in the lead. The streets are familiar now, so we are able to cut down the sandy lane that leads away from the house, and turn onto the gravel road, skirting the curves comfortably. We carry on, past the little square where the *boulangerie* and the market and the butcher are, buoyed by the wine and sugar and sense of abandon. When I turn back, I see Nina is not there. I stop. I call to the others to stop. We stagger still. And wait. She does not appear. She still does not appear. After a few minutes, I turn and ride back and find her. She is struggling with her bike. The strap of her purse slipped through the basket and caught in the wheel. "I fell off," she says. She points to her knee, where a bruise is forming. Even through the evening light, and the lush green, and the sugar and the oysters and the wine, I can feel the shards of anger and resentment. "You all just kept going!" she says.

"I came back," I say. "Give me the purse."

"I mean, I fall right off, and *you all just keep going.*"

So much past experience remains a present truth for so many of us, even when the present contradicts it at every turn. When the inciting incident in your life is having been left, by marriage, by family, by parents, by culture—by the person or place whose very role it is to hold you close—it is not something you overcome once and get on with afterward. It is something you are always overcoming. It is something you are always trying to get on afterward with. But maybe each time you overcome it more quickly. Maybe the wound does not pierce as deeply. Maybe when you're having a bad night of dancing in the Bois, for instance, on a trip that is meant to satisfy months of solitude, and you find yourself awkward and out of step as though you've dropped through a wormhole to your worst adolescent self, you only languish in it briefly before getting on to the afterward. Maybe when you fall off your bike after organizing a birthday dinner and are left behind, you let someone help.

We bike on, all together. In formation. Ellie in the front, singing Beyoncé as we go. Her phone held aloft as she tries to capture all of us in our organized flight.

Across the island we go. Until finally, in the setting sun, we reach the ancient stone citadel where the festival is. Around us are more people than I've seen all week. Dressed in goth outfits I haven't seen since high school. Small children race about. In the back area, stands selling food and wine. Inside, to the right, a stage, and to the left a large sandbox where young men (I only see young men, but it's dark) whip their BMX bikes around.

We purchase terrible white wine from a stand. The sort served at college parties.

And then Nicolas takes the stage. Nina corrals us all onto the dance floor and we compensate for the absence of anyone else.

Nicolas, shy and sweet in life, bursts onto the stage, screaming heavy metal lyrics I wouldn't understand even if they weren't in French. And we dance. *Do we dance.* We leap and flail and take up as much space as we can with our bodies. We want him to feel loved and celebrated. Here in this ancient citadel with the stone walls circling around us on a dark French island in the Atlantic. We remain like this for the entire set.

When we eventually leave, hours later; Sandra walks ahead, through the echoey, empty stone-walled arena and waits for us on the other side. She leans back and suddenly everything is flooded with light. "Oh god, I hit the light switch," she says, screaming with laughter. Before flicking it off again.

We bike home in the dark, the smell of the sea, calling to each other regularly like joyful foghorns to make sure no one has veered too far off. "No phones," I say. "Let's just use our brains!"

.   .   .

There are bells on Sunday. I neglect to count, but it seems like more than 186. I let them just be bells. Wash over me like the waves. Present and comforting in their consistency.

Sometime in the spring, when I wasn't going to Film Forum to take long siestas with Romy, I watched *Summertime* with Katharine Hepburn. In it, Hepburn plays Jane Hudson, an unmarried middle-aged woman on holiday in Venice who has a conflicted romance with a married Venetian shop owner. Hepburn was forty-seven when she filmed it. The same age I have just turned.

I came to *Summertime* with great optimism. After all, this was *Hepburn*. She had not removed herself from Hollywood for fear of age. Or any other fear. I had been watching her my whole life and she had never disappointed me.

And then I watched *Summertime*. And I hated it.

I hated that I hated it. But I *hated* it.

Where was the grown woman out in the world, bringing all her hard-won self-knowledge and experience to this adventure? Nowhere, was the answer. Instead, Hepburn's Jane Hudson was a Sabrina with more wrinkles. Insecure. Silly. A child in middle-aged clothes.

It felt to me like Hepburn, a woman who had flouted convention her entire life, was belittling herself. Kowtowing to some diminished idea of spinsterdom. Sad, innocent, pathetic, naive, underdeveloped.

And yet, some inadvertent truth had been captured. The mistaken but seemingly commonly held belief that when one is involved in the activities we associate with young women, one is experiencing them with the mind-set of a young woman. That only the exterior has changed.

Here on this island our enjoyment is filtered through the deaths of parents, the deaths of fiancés, cultural exclusion, shattering divorces, overwhelming financial uncertainty, the shouldering of life, and a bone-deep understanding of how to enjoy life, even when you're told how you do so can't possibly be satisfying in a real way. And then enjoying it anyway.

We don't have Nicolas's car to help us return the luggage to the ferry, so instead we agree that Ellie and I will attach the two carts we have to the bikes and make a number of round trips while everyone else cleans the house. This is ideal. Biking over cleaning. Is this what it's like to be the husband? Activity over drudgery? But not drudgery to those currently cleaning. I know that much. These are women who prize control, while all I ever do is yearn after momentum. These are women who know the time, at all times. They are never without a watch. The road to the harbor is downhill, and as Ellie and I come curving around the corner, into the center, Ellie raises her left hand in triumph. *On va Prendre!*

After the bikes are returned, we join the long line for the ferry back to the mainland. I'm surprised there are this many people on the island; it had seemed practically empty this entire time. There are so many that once we board we can't get seats together. There are no dolphins on this crossing, just large rollicking waves.

The train back is delayed. This is very French. Trains are always being delayed. Ellie tries to find out what our options are as the rest of us sit on the ground, our backs against our bags, as though we've returned to being teenage backpackers who stay in hostels.

The train is coming. The train is not coming. Now a bus is coming. Clouds of black birds swoop overhead as the sun sets, swarming together in a tree in the square, giving off a great racket. A murder of crows? An unkindness of ravens? A joyful of women on holiday?

Eventually a bus arrives to take us to Nantes, where we can catch a train back to Paris. We secure the front seats and roll through the French countryside under the sliver of a moon. Who lives in these low houses, I wonder. What do they do?

We make a rushed farewell at Montparnasse. Tomorrow is Monday, and for Aarti and Ellie that means back to the office. I Vélib' home through a dark but lively Paris. *Les vacances* have ended. The Parisians are back. As I cross Saint-Michel on Saint-Germain, I hear singing coming from a group under the lamp outside the café. It sounds like hymns.

FIFTEEN

Oui, Monsieur

After many exchanges of messages, I finally connect with the person I have taken to referring to as Le Spanker.

I begin to compose the experience in my head to tell the others, even as it's happening. I have already told them where I am going. Given them the address. The name I know him as. A photo.

"I'm making him meet me downstairs!" I say, in response to Sandra's concerned "Make sure to check in when you leave." The reliable network of women keeping eyes trained on one another.

When we make the plan to meet, he asks what kind of wine I drink. He wants me to come straight up, meet him directly in his apartment, but I'm too American for that. At dinner the other night, Henri, a Parisian friend of Nina's who I once went dancing with at a gay club where naked men stood in glass boxes and rubbed themselves down with soapy sponges, hears me describing how the men on these apps keep asking me to leave the door open, to be lying on the bed, and says, "It's common now.

"I met with a woman who was waiting on the bed blindfolded," he says. "I wasn't allowed to speak and she didn't want to know what I looked like."

"Aren't they concerned about safety?" I ask.

A very French shrug. "There are no serial killers in France."

I have no idea if this is true, but as Nina scathingly interjects, "It only takes one."

I'm far too much of a New Yorker, or North American, or raised on a culture of television about female corpses, to overcome this. Meeting at my own apartment is one thing. But I need a meet-and-greet drink before entering someone else's. Which is what I insist on before agreeing to make the trek up here.

"That's fine," is his short response over Fruitz. I can sense the extremely French dismissiveness through my screen. I hear the words with a haughty accent.

I know the Parisians have returned from their holiday because there are more cars on the street. But the bike lane up Boulevard de Magenta, after I skirt République, is the first place that reminds me Paris is not my home. I no longer have it to myself. Even when there are tourists in Paris they don't tend to bike up here, so often in August I can fly all the way up this busy boulevard and not have to navigate around too many people. No more. Whatever part of my brain that has been released these past weeks to tangle *en français* with verbs and phrases and sometimes entire conversations gets snatched back to deal with the weaves and the brakes and the bells on the narrow bike lane that is separated from a sidewalk of pedestrians by a faint line and some implicit agreement. By the time I arrive on the edges of the 17th it's as though I have just stepped off the plane at CDG. My French has disappeared.

I haven't been to this neighborhood before. When I come up to the 17th it's usually farther over in Batignolles. I'm west of that now. The Paris of locals. The Paris that, if it empties out in August, only does so for one week. The people who live here don't have country houses. Tonight the cafés are full, spilling out onto the sidewalks like someone has overturned a bucket of small toys.

I'm five minutes late. Which I feel is shockingly punctual for a first meet-up. I spot him at a table outside the café, slim and erect.

He looks like his photo, I will say to the group—handsome, tall, erect, like a well-cut suit—but sterner than his messages.

I can feel him assessing me.

"You are five minutes late." No smile. I can sense a slender iron rod running through his words. His accent is very thick. Thick as though he's been cast by Hollywood to play a Frenchman in a film written by an American writer.

He is very, very French, I will say. If you could turn the formal *vous* into a person, it would be him.

"My Google Maps sent me down the wrong street," I say lightheartedly, already irritated with myself for giving an excuse. And a little fascinated at the same time. I'm not used to such direct anger.

He nods. No smile.

I'm never more aware of how much time I spend with expats in

Paris than when I come up against a real Parisian. The internet has dulled geographies down somewhat, like everywhere—a New York accent is mostly a thing of the past now, for instance. Someone once told me the reason so many young French people (and presumably others) speak English is because of *Game of Thrones*. But the famous French haughtiness still exists. I am facing a furnace of it right now.

Any hope that the French that I lost on the ride up here will suddenly make a comeback evaporates in the face of this actual *Frenchness*. I can barely squeak out, *"Un verre de rosé."* In fact, the server asks me to repeat myself three times until Le Spanker steps in and orders for me with a . . . is it a smirk?

It's not a smirk, exactly, but I feel like I catch an exchange of looks between him and the server. They're not wrong. Up here, in this crowd, I can feel myself give off tourist energy.

(Ellie tells me the problem is my accent, not that I am using the wrong words. This is comforting to a degree, though I suspect that is not currently the issue.)

The prospect of his apartment, just two doors down and up some stairs, hangs over us. This feels like a very strange sort of interview. For the first time this summer I feel like an applicant.

I ask him what he does. He tells me he's a gym teacher. I immediately imagine him standing on the side of fields, some sort of stick in hand, barking orders. All our exchanges until now have been charming. Fun. Forward. Unlike a number of other men I have matched with whose messages have clearly been put through Google Translate: their descriptions of what they intend to do to my "clitoris" make me think I'm making an appointment for a gynecological exam. This was notably the case with one personal trainer I exchanged some pleasantries with. His messages to me were accompanied by a video of him naked and oiled up; his body looked as though it might have been the model for Michelangelo's *David*, but his language was so clinical I couldn't quite get past it.

Le Spanker, however, has demonstrated in every message a real proficiency with English. Which it turns out he does not have. Nor the sense of humor, it seems. He struggles to find the words in English he wants, and when I help him, I just get a curt nod, as though I have spoken out of turn. Again, I find myself fascinated. What is the translation app he's been using, I wonder. I'm reminded of a man I was involved with years ago, whose proficiency with grammar in his texts charmed me almost as much as what he was texting (sometimes more). The extra time he was taking with those commas and semicolons felt like their own sort of love letter. It was only later it occurred to me he just had the highest level of autocorrect turned on on his phone. The deception of language, the truth of body language.

"Do you actually write your messages to me?" I ask, the way one might ask whether you prefer olive oil or butter when cooking, trying to sort out whether his written English is just far superior to his spoken or if he has some assistance. What's the secret? I'm actually just curious. It's not like I have much of a language leg to stand on here. I see immediately that I've offended him. I elaborate, to show that it was a sincerely meant question, I just stumbled through a basic drink order, after all. "I just mean, do you write it directly or do you use some sort of translation?"

"I write it," he says, eyes blazing, as if I've suggested he's illiterate entirely.

"Amazing," I say, trying to redirect the conversation. "Your English

is so good." A shrug. "I wish I could say the same about my French."
Another shrug.

I finish my wine.

He asks: "Will we go up?"

I could leave now. Easily. I can say no, get on a Vélib', meet one of
the women for a drink, have one by myself. I'm not lacking options.

But I don't want to. I'm intrigued. I want to see what happens.

This "see what happens" inclination goes against centuries of training; I can feel them like dominos threatening to fall against my desire. Women who "see what happens" are asking for it. The outcome
is almost always deadly, or shameful, or both. Women who are asking
for it are always alone. That is their downfall. Alone, disconnected,
removed from the pack. Vulnerable to be hunted.

But I am *actually* asking for it. I have literally asked for this. And
based on all our exchanges, I have a good sense of what I'm asking for.
And yet, it's very difficult to understand the act of asking as anything
other than a request for punishment. The nonconsensual kind. It takes
resolve to see it otherwise.

Also, even if I am by myself right now, I am hardly alone. I move
about the world with an international shadow company of people on
my side. Near and far.

Up we go.

His apartment consists of a narrow living room. And equally narrow kitchen to one side, and to the left another door that I assume
goes to the bedroom. One wall of the living room is floor-to-ceiling
books, facing it is a couch, where I sit. He opens a bottle of white wine
and pours me a glass.

"You said you wanted white," he says, and I wonder if some expression on my face suggested otherwise.

"Yes, thank you."

"I'm a writer too," he says, standing before me, books behind him.

Oh god, here we go.

"What sort of writer?"

He reviews heavy metal music for an indie music magazine. He tells me this without a shred of irony.

"Amazing," I say. He picks up a guitar. He has not asked me where I write for, which is a relief. I have found you can either talk about yourself, or write about yourself, but doing both is a bit much. He turns and puts some music on. It takes my ear a while to adjust but eventually I realize it's some sort of metal band covering Fleetwood Mac. He has still not smiled once since I arrived.

"What's the last album you reviewed?"

He stands there with his glass of wine, looking down at me, and starts to describe it. I have no idea what he's talking about, which doesn't seem to faze him.

"Do you want more wine?" I hold up the bottle.

"You interrupted me," he says.

I lean back and realize the anger, all the vocabulary around "punishment" is not a kink. It's a personality.

"Is it anger or insecurity?" I will later ask Ellie.

"What's the difference?" she says.

I have more wine. What am I looking for here exactly? Something new. Some new way to feel and be seen. But also, there is some appeal in being told what to do. I am the only person who tells me what to do most days. I've spent this trip telling people what I want and when I want it. A brief vacation from me is appealing. As if delegating it is service I have availed myself of. A relinquishment of control in a life where I possess an enormous amount. It's also a novelty. What is it like to take orders? I take orders from almost no one. Literally. I work for myself. I live alone. I come and go largely on my own schedule.

Surely, if I bothered to look, I could probably find reams of feminist theory on domination and whether one can be a feminist and still, at moments, enjoy being told what to do. I assume this has been argued over and pulled apart. And discussed at length. And for good reason. For a long time and still in many places women don't have any other way to be than to follow orders. If you are a woman who's finally escaped that, what does it mean to be attracted to it, even just in the bedroom? I am touristing in the land of asking permission.

But it's more too. Giving instructions can take thought. Thought about me. Every move I make is a focal point of another person. There is intention to all this. Someone is paying attention. There is a wild visibility that comes with all these instructions, which I'm unaccustomed to.

But, at the moment, I'm not terribly interested in using this brief rendezvous as a judgment on my own feminism. So far I'm enjoying myself. That is good enough for me. Anyway, if you summon a loss of control, is it actually a loss of control? Or is it just another way to be in charge.

He sits on the couch beside me. His anger feels like a physical presence. But also a certainty. There is, at all times, something appealing about a person who knows exactly what they want.

"My face is off limits," I say.

He was very into spanking, I'll tell people later. I'll be surprised by how many times the response is, "Oh, I love a good spanking."

For the next five days whenever I sit down, at dinner or on a Vélib', I will be reminded of that evening. The aftermath of extreme sensation being more sensation.

"You left marks," I will message him a day or two later after catching my reflection in the mirror when I get out of the shower.

"Oops I did it again," is the response.

This is part of the thrill for him, I'm sure. Some sort of branding. I was here, do not forget it. But for me it's simply proof I was seen. Nothing more. After what felt like such a long time of being unseen, that I carry evidence otherwise is, for now anyway, still a thrill for me.

I am here. My body exists in the world.

SIXTEEN

I Do Believe I've Had Enough

think a lot about narrative structure. I suppose this is what happens when enough people tell you your story is not worthy of one. I have a theory about how we understand narrative: I've come to wonder whether our adherence to the three-act structure—setup, confrontation, resolution—is simply based on the male orgasm.

No really, think about it.

Tension, execution, release. The end.

This makes sense. Men have written most of our history. The proof is right there in the spelling. And why wouldn't the story be based on their most primal, most desired experience?

The notion that women should expect to experience pleasure during sex is a relatively new one in Western culture (there's no question plenty of women *did*, just that they were not expected to, nor *should* expect to). Sex, instead, was often something to be endured. Believed to be an obligation to endure. The female orgasm, for many women, elusive, and often more complicated to achieve. Even now studies (and quite a few women's magazine articles intent on solving this dilemma) suggest a shocking number of women do not experience orgasm during sex. It takes more work, more patience. It's more complicated.

What would a story arc based on the female orgasm look like. Like waves, I imagine. Some bigger and more significant than others, some smaller and gentler, in no particular order. I don't think it's unrealistic to say many women experience their best orgasms at their own hands. The narrative of pleasure for women often being a solo one. The inciting incident a hand taken to oneself, the tension, the release, but then, if you know your body well enough, understand what you like and what you want, more again. Perhaps with more intensity, perhaps with less. But on it goes. The highs of varying degrees, the lows too. Neither permanent. To be enjoyed, or endured, with the knowledge that everything ends, and also everything begins. Perhaps the crisis point happens in the middle of the story. Perhaps the inciting incident is just that you liked it and you want more, and you can have more. That, in fact, we exist outside the timeline we have been strapped to.

The climax of my weeks in Paris happened midway through my time there, during my Sunday walk through the empty city alongside the procession of nuns with the terrible news from Kabul coming through my phone. It was weeks before I understood it as such, and only then did it begin to loop backward and forward, arching over the whole trip, giving structure to how I would come to think about my time in

Paris. I return to that walk again and again. Sliding through it as I move back and forth through my own story.

I had come to Paris because I could no longer be alone. I needed to be seen. And touched. And loved.

I came because I knew what I needed, and I knew how to get it, and then I did.

I came because, for all my talk of money and budgets and savings, I knew my own value and I understood how best to spend myself.

I came because I could.

Because is a loaded word that leads down many avenues. Like the roundabouts I navigate through Paris, with each exit beginning in the same place and then shooting off in a wildly different direction. I came here because I lead a life that lets me move around and still work. I came because I hold the passport that allows me to pass through most borders easily. I came because even though I don't have a lot of money, I have enough. I came because I had spent years cultivating a life here and the roots had gone deep enough that life was still waiting for me after I had left it for longer than I intended.

But there were larger *becauses* too. No amount of enjoyment can stem the awareness that this sort of movement, the picking up and dropping into another place, is increasingly fraught. The planet is rejecting our cavalier excursions. And so, part of the reason I came is not just because it had recently been impossible, but because I am aware it might not be possible for that much longer.

And then there was the largest *because*.

On that quiet Sunday walk across Paris, midway through my trip, body sore from pleasure, I was bracketed by two versions of how most stories for women have almost always gone. To my right were the nuns. The centuries-old tale of how women survived outside marriage and motherhood. On my phone, the news from Kabul and the familiar and ever-advancing story of women being driven back into the place men preferred them to be: behind closed doors, where every movement and decision requires permission. All action in service to a central character, which as history tells us, is never the woman.

Then there was me. Wedged between the two. A woman alone. A woman who wasn't required to ask permission. Who could do as she pleased. I was the anomaly, where history was concerned. They were the norm.

Of course, I only appear to be alone. I am about as far from alone as Greta Garbo was when she left the great storytelling machine of Hollywood. I am merely one of many choosing to live like this, so much so that it feels absurd to even have to say so.

And yet, somehow, I feel compelled to note it because this story of women doing what they want is so new no one is quite sure how to tell yet.

Would we get the chance to figure it out? I sometimes wonder if I were an alien who could look at all of human history—past, present, and future—would I see the life I'm living and all the choices I get to make as progress, or a would I view it as a blip, a narrow strip of time, before everything inevitably reverts back to the way it had almost always been?

And if it turned out I *was* a blip, traversing a narrow strip of possibility between centuries of reality—a brief moment in time we'd quickly forget about, one that would take on fabulist proportions as it disappeared behind us—then all I could think was at least I knew enough to walk down that street, so to speak, while I was able to. We're frequently reminded there is no greater sin a woman can commit than to take great pleasure in herself. But at least I was smart enough not to feel bad about doing so.

In the end I had come because I knew enough to enjoy myself.

This was not knowledge I had acquired in these weeks; it was not my reward for taking a risk and leaving home. It was knowledge I possessed, was reminded of, and put to use. Over and over again.

I never end up seeing the Masseur. My first Fruitz match who, after all those months in New York spent alone dreaming of hands on my body, set me on fire with his language of caress: *indulgente* and *très gentil*. The person who had forced me to consider why I was here in the first place. He finally returns to Paris just before I'm scheduled to depart. I have been touched quite a lot since we first connected, but what he has in mind still sounds nice and one afternoon during my last week in Paris, I walk to the address he's given me in the 13th. This is another living Paris neighborhood. Few tourists come here even in the high months. It's quiet. Charming but less grand. I make some turns and finally come to his corner. I double-check the address. I don't particularly like the look of his building. It stands alone. Exposed. Some of the shutters on the windows askew. Nope. This is not for me. I turn around without a second thought. I know what I don't want too. And I don't want this. I realize I'd already gotten everything I needed from him when I arrived. I message him that I can't make it after all, and then walk down to the café at the Grande Mosquée de Paris and order myself a sweet tea and a *brick à l'oeuf.* When I'm finished, I cross the street and sit down in the Jardin des Plantes and watch all the passersby in the golden light.

The day before I leave Paris, I go to take the mandatory Covid test required to allow me to board the plane. Plans have already been made in case I test positive, which seems not unlikely. I have tested regularly while here, but still, fun is not free; they that dance must pay the fiddler; flying too close to the sun, etc. Apartments have been sourced in case I need to quarantine. Groceries will be delivered to me. It will be fine, I'm assured. The pleasure of others' concern is added onto the pile of all the other pleasures I have experienced this month.

I test negative.

At some point this wave of good fortune will end. At some point I will be once again in the valley of uncertainty with walls rising up on either side. And it will seem deep and at times insurmountable. But that too will end. For now, I simply ride on. This fortune's favorite life will last as long as it will last, and I will let it carry me as far as it can.

On my bike ride home from my last supper with Nina and Sandra and Aarti and Ellie I come rolling across the Seine, still in my red Monoprix dress. I pass a handsome young French man—he looks like a newly returned student, also on a bike, on the opposite side of the boulevard. He gives me an open smile of youth. A few minutes later he pulls up beside me, out of breath from turning around and trying to catch up. *"Bonsoir,"* he says. *"Très gentile,"* he says. And then he asks in French if he can ride with me home. I don't need a translator.

I consider the offer. I can say yes. I can take him and his youth and his open smile with me and enjoy it. It is entirely up to me.

I complain all the time about how nearly every story involving women ends with a wedding or a baby. But it's not true. In *Sweet Charity*, Shirley MacLaine is ditched by her lover at the City Hall altar. Destroyed, she wanders through Central Park, falling asleep on a bench, until she is woken by a group of hippies (including a sweet, open-faced Bud Cort) who give her flowers and wish her peace. Revived, she gets up, shakes herself off, and marches off down Fifth Avenue. "And she lived hopefully ever after," the credits tell us. The higher-ups were nervous about this and made director Bob Fosse film an alternate, "happier" ending, one in which her fiancé returns and all is well. These execs were worried that audiences wouldn't react well to Charity's solo fate. But when both were completed and they compared them, they went with the original, agreeing it was the superior of the two. Hopefully over happily.

I thank my open-faced, handsome companion and tell him I must decline.

"Désolé," he says, and blows me a kiss as he turns around and bikes back in the other direction.

I love Paris, but it is not my home. It is a mirror that has allowed me to see my entire self, and I have spent these weeks taking enormous pleasure in the wholeness of that person. But New York is calling and it's time to go. I have had enough.

For now.

Acknowledgments

Thank you to Lucy Carson and Amy Sun for believing in this project and seeing it through with such care. Thanks to Ann for the accountability. To Naama, Miriam, Laura, and Jo, for the early reads. To Kimberly, Lesley, Jenn, Marisa, and Rachel. And, as always, to Jen, Maureen, Carolyn, Michelle, Maris, and Kate for the regular group therapy and support.